Living the Season

Living the Season

ZEN PRACTICE FOR TRANSFORMATIVE TIMES

JI HYANG PADMA

QUEST BOOKS

Theosophical Publishing House
Wheaton, Illinois * Chennai, India

Quest Books
P. O. Box 270
Wheaton, IL 60187-0270

www.questbooks.net

Cover image: Leungchopan/Shutterstock
Cover design by Greta Polo

Library of Congress Cataloging-in-Publication Data

Padma, Ji Hyang.
  Living the season: Zen practice for transformative times
/ Ji Hyang Padma.—First Quest edition.
    pages   cm
Includes index.
ISBN 978-0-8356-0919-7
1. Spiritual life—Zen Buddhism. I. Title.
BQ9288.P33   2013
294.3′444—dc23   2013007589

          5 4 3 2 1 * 13 14 15 16 17 18

        Printed in the United States of America

CONTENTS

Contents

Contents

ACKNOWLEDGMENTS

First of all, I am grateful for the gift of my spiritual teachers and mentors: Zen Master Seung Sahn, Maha Ghosananda, Zen Master Dae Bong, Sonia Choquette, Don Francisco Chura Flores, and Steven Encinas.

Thank you to my spiritual friends, especially Cheryl Perreault, Brett Bevell, Kate Lila Wheeler, Algernon D'Ammassa, Ani Ngawang Tendol, and the nuns of Keydong Thuk-Che-Cho-Ling for their creative inspiration and support along the path.

Thank you also to the meditation circles at Wellesley College, Grozier Road, and Omega Institute. Through their great vow may compassion and wisdom arise to the benefit of all beings.

INTRODUCTION

We are collectively going through a time of complete transformation: *kairos*, a turning moment. To the Greeks, kairos referred to the sacred and vital nature of time, a choice point in which we must seize the opportunity as it arises. We are faced with kairos now: the gifts—as well as necessity—of being able to turn around some of the desecration of our sacred earth. We have the potential to shift from a culture of competition and marketing-driven hunger to a culture of sustainability and cooperation. The earth requires our awakening and compassionate action for a future to be possible.

Fortunately, Zen practice provides a grounding and centering force through which we can find calm abiding in the middle of the storm. There are prophecies for times of great change across the world's indigenous traditions. Many people know about the Mayan prophecy—a prophecy often misconstrued. Conventional wisdom would have had its effects take place upon a single day. However, that time cycle spans millennia; therefore the

1

transition is still with us. If we look at the environmental crisis, economic systems, and other global systems that have shown fraying at the seams, then it is clear that this is, absolutely, a turning point. In the Hindu tradition, which served as a spiritual foundation for the Buddha, there is also such a prophecy. The *Kali Yuga*, which dates back roughly thirty-five hundred years, indicates we are within a long phase of complete transformation.

This prophecy is referenced within Buddhism by the Lotus Sutra. The Lotus Sutra describes the Kali Yuga as a time of great change—what Zen students call "hard training"—when people will need actively and intentionally to connect with their inner wisdom and act with alignment and integrity. Without this connection to source, people may act against the grain of their true nature and experience tumult and struggle. At this point, a core teaching is brought forth, which is also a charge we are given to meet these changing times: the Lion's Roar.

The Lion's Roar is a practice of complete openness. By moving toward our experience and seeing everything that arises as workable, we have access to the highest energy—complete fearlessness. We find ourselves in the middle of the sacred circle of our life without anything left out: everything is rich material for awakening. Through meditation, we come into alignment with the wild energies within our own mind. Having established inner equilibrium, we deepen our meditation practice through engagement with everyday life. While there are some rough waters we are encountering collectively—shifts in the global economy, the limits of consumption-based economic growth, and the immense challenges to our ecosystem, among others— we can navigate these rushing rivers by working skillfully with the patterns of our life. As Zen Master Thich Nhat Hanh notes:

> In Vietnam, there are many people, called boat people, who leave the country in small boats. Often the boats are caught in rough seas or storms, the people may panic, and boats can sink. But if even one person can remain calm, lucid, knowing what to do and what not to do, he or she can help the boat survive. His or her expression—face, voice—communicates clarity and calmness, and people have trust in that person. They will listen to what he or she says. One person can save the lives of many. Our world is something like a small boat.[1]

The practices I share in this book will help you to be that person and to bring your awareness and compassion to full expression in this changing world. This is the essence of leadership: using all resources at hand so that your own presence itself calms the storms and all beings can experience safety and well-being. This begins with our own readiness to come into alignment with the wild energies of our own body/mind.

The practices I share are based on a core experience of wholeness. In Zen, we take a position of radical inclusivity: we see that all energies within the Self are workable. Every element brings unique gifts. To quote from the eighth-century poem "Sandokai": "Fire heats, wind moves, water wets, earth is solid." When we are at home with these elemental energies, every season is a good season. For that reason, I have organized the practice chapters of this book around the four seasons.

We will begin with winter. Many people are experiencing the current economic climate as a time of scarcity—a time of seeking shelter from the wind, when the natural world brings forth fewer leaves and branches. Yet, even in the midst of winter, there is life. Tree sap quickens and begins to flow beneath the surface bark. Birds graze where the ice thaws. We see the prints of foraging deer, otter, and raccoons. In the dark soil underneath the blanket of snow, seeds are stirring. The quiet of winter prepares the ground for spring.

As we come out of stillness, replenished at our roots, new life emerges. We open our windows to let in the fragrance of blossoms. Shoots green with life force emerge from the earth. As these shoots ripen, the days become longer and the breeze more gentle. Beauty surrounds us;

this fullness of life is summer. The leaves unfurl, roses and irises open; we play in the divine garden.

This fullness is followed by a season of harvest, of pressing the sweetness of summer into wine through our skillful action in the world. In autumn, we give thanks for the gifts we have been given. As the sap returns back to the roots of the trees, the unseen side of nature, our inner processes, are nurtured. Again, we find true happiness through practices of spaciousness and letting go. In another season, this open space will give rise to new beginnings. In the words of Zen Master Wu-Men:

> Spring comes with flowers, autumn with the moon,
> Summer with breeze, winter with snow.
> When idle concerns don't hang in your mind,
> That is your best season.[2]

My own practice, across the span of twenty-some years, has shown me that our energies ebb and flow like the tides; they wax and wane like the moon. The endings that we experience are also the beginning of something else. This is the source of our renewal and a lasting happiness, which is not dependent on conditions. When we engage fully with these natural rhythms—the stillness of winter and the passionate activity of summer—we join the general dance that is the life force expressing itself through us. In these rhythms, we sense our deep connection to all living things: a wholeness both within and all around us. When we touch that wholeness, we are healed and restored; we uncover our inner resources. This is the path that I invite you to share with me, through an exploration of the foundations of Zen practice, and then through the journey of this book through the four seasons.

In order to place this in its fullest context so that this practice of radical openness to our life can be fully appreciated, embodied, and practiced in moment-to-moment life, I will begin by describing the connectedness of our body/mind and the wisdom of its kinesthetic awareness.

EMBODIED KNOWING

Through the emerging field of interpersonal neurology, we know that early experiences of safety and connection prime our responses to our world and shape our own capacity for emotional self-regulation. The openness and presence of parents, holding space for their child without interfering, is what makes it possible for that child, and then the adult, to be present with his or her own experience without feeling overwhelmed and without suppressing the vitality of a full-bodied, affective life.[3]

Throughout our lives, that quality of presence and unconditional acceptance continues to be the greatest gift we can receive or give. When we extend this deep listening to ourselves and others, we touch a place of wholeness, clarity, and well-being. Through the practices that I will introduce in the following chapters, we can gain greater ease and grace in bringing the mind home to its innate clarity. This sense of resiliency, deep connectedness, and happiness not based on conditions is our natural state. We'll explore this territory together through the diverse realms of ancient and contemporary spiritual practices.

ORIGINS: THE WAY-SEEKING MIND

For me, this path became clear through trusting my own wholeness—touching a place of deep wholeness within, and also sensing how that felt experience brought me into relationship with my life, all sentient beings, and this natural world.

Throughout my teenage years, I felt a natural restlessness and that my search for meaning needed to break new ground. At the age of fourteen, I'd witnessed a car crash: a sedan meeting a Trans-Am, fiberglass flying everywhere. At that moment, I felt frozen in limbic overwhelm. In the next moment, I broke free from that impasse and ran to call an ambulance.

That moment catalyzed a new level of self-awareness. My intention to be of help in that moment met with an unruly, somato-emotional reality. The limbic feeling of being overwhelmed had nearly prevented me from helping these people in a critical moment. I recognized the need to get training to be able to respond in a way that would truly be of help.

Work on a volunteer ambulance at the age of seventeen deepened my spiritual quest. Through our teamwork, we were able to intervene in all kinds of medical crises, alleviating suffering and protecting lives. Even within this meaningful and exciting work, I found my ability to be of service limited by the sphere of an EMT's work. CPR only works in one of four or five cases at best. After forty minutes of working intensively on someone's body, we would then need to call a time of death and report to the family that there is nothing else we can do.

Within the work of an EMT, the best glimpse of the miracle of life is revealed within emergency childbirth. When there is the opportunity and need to assist with emergency childbirth in the field, mother and child often know just what to do, and a child appears in the world, bright eyed with a life of possibility ahead. In the call I served on, the emergency childbirth took place at a local high school; the mother was a teenager and not excited about becoming a mother. The nature of EMT work is that we share just that one moment in time. What lay ahead for this tiny family over the next week—or over the intervening years—we don't know. While it is the nature of mind to resist that fundamental insecurity—that we cannot grasp the future—EMT work is good training in letting go. We have *just this moment*.

More often, the calls we received were not so dramatic. For example, a senior at the nursing home had ripped out the feeding tube in her stomach, not wishing to continue the marginal existence this provided. We would then transport the patient to the hospital, the hospital would reinsert the feeding tube, and we would then transport the elder back to the nursing home. This cycle would repeat, often with the same patient; it can be clearly seen that these transports were not producing any lasting benefit. In this way, I felt a strong calling to look into the roots of these issues: what is suffering and how do we alleviate it?

These questions, this path, continued in college. In college, I took up aikido, a martial art of bringing energies into harmony—our own vital energies as well as the energies of those we encounter. This provided some very tangible ways of alleviating suffering by reconciling opposing energies through movement that was exquisitely beautiful and profoundly effective. With this practice, I began for the first time to get to know my own body as sacred space through which I was always in dialogue with people and the environment.

This kinesthetic, dynamic, tangible experience of my own spirit when I was a young Wellesley student turned my world around. I felt the energies of heaven and earth blend through my movements and became aware of this embodied knowing as a source of self-awareness, creativity, and instantaneous wisdom.

Through aikido, I was introduced to Zen shiatsu, a traditional Japanese acupressure-based bodywork that yokes together mind, body, and spirit. The flow between these modalities is considerable. With enough aikido practice—hours of tumbling onto straw tatami mats—the need for shiatsu becomes clear. In my case, I was fortunate to find a shiatsu teacher within our aikido community. Through his patient and compassionate teaching, I discovered the wisdom path within shiatsu. In Zen shiatsu, the core philosophy is that the body/mind is one whole *bodymind*, which possesses a natural ability to heal itself.

When we align clearly with natural rhythms, the body/mind comes into balance. Zen shiatsu supports this natural process. In the moment of diagnosis, the practitioner is sensing the client's imbalance and sharing that experience. This can be felt through the subtle movements of the abdomen, the muscles along the spine, and the timbre of the whole parasympathetic nervous system as it is met by the practitioner's empathetic, balanced response. The client's *bodymind* senses this touch-and-response as an experience of spontaneity, presence, and wholeness—which invites their whole self to restore its relationship and realign through the natural rhythms of the body with all that they are.

Through these modalities, it felt quite natural to enter Zen meditation practice. My greatest mentors in shiatsu and aikido had active meditation practices. As I prepared for a big aikido test, I knew my ability to be present and spontaneous in the moment would be thoroughly challenged. Meditation would help me to move from my core (called the *hara* in aikido) to respond from a place of centeredness, *ki* (vital energy), and personal power. That semester, I was also a senior in college, facing the uncertainties every senior faces: what career path should I choose, what happens next? These questions were urgently with me in 1990 as we faced a job market not unlike the climate that is pressing upon graduates right now. So I began Zen practice in this goal-oriented way: to reduce stress and strengthen my aikido practice. In Zen training, we practice unconditional awareness of the moment, just as it is. From that perspective, this goal-orientation is a mistake. And yet, so many of us do begin with a goal, so that is no problem. As we give ourselves over to this practice completely, it transforms us. It has certainly brought me through many transformations.

In those first weeks of practice, my mind and body became one; settling onto the cushion, I met myself right where I was. Sometimes the meditation was spacious and light; sometimes the energies that surfaced were painful, and tears flowed. However, throughout all of these experiences, it felt as if I were truly coming home.

At that moment when I took the aikido test, everything flowed seamlessly. My attention was centered in my hara. As my partner attacked, my responses were coordinated with his movement, redirecting his energy into the arcs of movement known as *ukemi*, the art of taking a fall. Through meditation practice, I was able to relax at this essential time so that my body remained supple, and the life force of my breath brought power into each movement. Immediately after, during the evening of celebration, the denouement of the test, I started feeling restless, and a new, inescapable question arose: *what is this for?*

It was very clear that the aikido test was not actually the purpose of this practice. So then, what was it about? That question kept me awake through the night. The next morning, I went to the Zen center's morning practice for the first time and began practicing in earnest. Meditation shifted from a focus upon external goals to a focus upon self-insight: *what am I?*

Upon graduation from Wellesley in 1991, I moved into the Zen center. The path was clear. This practice offered me a way of knowing myself and being of service, which could translate into compassionate action in day-to-day life.

So I lived at the Zen center, helping my teacher with Zen center community-building, and also took a job as an office manager at an acupuncture clinic for people with AIDS. Through this, I saw the effectiveness of meditation in helping people overcome physical suffering.

At the time, AIDS therapies were still primitive. Acupuncture helped ameliorate the side effects of AZT and other drugs and in supporting the immune system, but it was not curing anything. When I met these clients at their intakes, I found that many were young men, well dressed, asymptomatic, and quite personable. Over the intervening months, at some point a lesion might appear upon their arm or in another visible place upon the body; they would experience their first bout of pneumonia or a drop in weight; and from there, the immune system would inexorably and painfully take a downward dive. I had befriended many of these young clients, and they were dying in front of me. The question came up again: what is suffering and how do we alleviate it? The one thing I was able to do of direct benefit was practice: cultivate my own practice so that I could be compassionate and clear, and teach meditation to patients so that the upwelling of compassion and clarity could calm their fears by revealing their own inner resources.

At the same time, working with these AIDS patients, I became aware that life is short. The direction to be of service felt quite urgent in the face of their suffering. I decided to travel to Korea, sit a ninety-day intensive retreat, and ordain as a nun. The process of ordination commonly is preceded by an extended period of special training in temple life; out of the urgency that I felt for this work, I requested and was granted permission to ordain upon the completion of this intensive. For me, this was the most complete and direct response to the *koan* (question) of human suffering, the most skillful route to healing this world.

The retreat took place at Shin Won Sah, a temple on Kye Ryong San, a sacred mountain in South Korea. Practice began in early November and continued until early February. Each day, the schedule was the same: wake at 3:00 a.m., begin practice with 108 prostrations at 3:20 a.m., then chant and sit throughout the day until 9 p.m. During the second half of the retreat, I added midnight practice—waking at 11:30 p.m., practicing until 1:30 a.m. The intensity of practice acts as a forge, heating and strengthening mind and heart. One's dedication is tested by the rigors of practice, culture shock, and the tightness of body that accrues with long sitting. The testing was profoundly useful, as it revealed the places where my practice lagged. On an intensive retreat, there is no escape from the practice: the only possible response is to heat up the heart, which would be necessary for life as a monastic in the West.

In order to ordain, one has to want to do so one hundred percent. Ninety percent is too little, one hundred ten percent, too much. It is an issue if people are holding back, somewhat uncommitted inside; it is equally an issue in Zen training if people are fervently overeager, as that suggests that they have not completely integrated the process. Across three months, I began to know myself more deeply, and my own karma (mind habits).

Although practice was not always easy, the retreat confirmed my vow to awaken and help others awaken. At the end of the retreat, I received nun's precepts from Zen Master Seung Sahn at Hwa Gye Sah temple in Seoul. With these precepts, I also received a new name and new role. The name I was given is Ji Hyang. "Ji" means wisdom; "Hyang" means fragrance. The name is traditionally given based on what Dharma, what inner truth, the teacher sees within the novice as their potential.

In Zen we describe the evolution of our practice using the word "direction," as our way is a path of continuous practice, which continues ten thousand years, nonstop, together with all beings. Even the Buddha, if he were alive, would still be practicing to completely attain the way. This name given to me at ordination, Ji Hyang, helped me to more completely step into this role.

At the end of the retreat, while preparing to return to the West, I asked Zen Master Seung Sahn, "I have just taken precepts. What advice would you give me?" He replied, "Only do it!" When we wholeheartedly connect to the Bodhisattva Vow to pay attention and be of service, each situation is our teacher; each situation provides us with the means to awaken. I returned to the Cambridge Zen Center to resume training under my teacher there and accepted the position of Zen center director.

As director, I was the primary staff member involved in publicity, outreach, and creating community for one of the largest Zen centers in the country—and through these years, the Zen center experienced strong growth. The creative aspects of this work were tangible as well as deeply rewarding.

In 1997, I accepted the position of Cambridge Zen Center Abbot, a larger assignment that served as a vehicle to express my deep love for this practice, and to give myself even more fully to the Sangha, the community—as well as possessing its unique challenges. The Abbot oversees all administrative functions of the Zen center: three buildings, thirteen ongoing classes, thirty hours a week of practice offered to the community, and a residential Zen training program that was, at forty-five people, at full capacity.

In Buddhism, we speak of Three Treasures: Buddha, referring to our original nature; Dharma, the teaching; and Sangha, the community. Of these, it is often said, "One begins practice out of love for Buddha or Dharma; what one gets is Sangha." During these five years, my energies were devoted to our collective attaining of Sangha. Residential community practice is a strong practice of letting go, perceiving the situation clearly, and living together harmoniously. Practicing together, working together, experiencing the ten thousand joys and sorrows together, one at last recognizes nonduality. If someone is happy, I am happy; if someone is sad, I am sad. There is no separation. The vow to save all beings is simultaneously a deep gratitude to all beings for already having saved me.

At the same time, as anyone who has served in this capacity can attest, serving as Abbot and caring for the administration of a Zen center can sometimes lead us back into the thickets of the modern professional life with its spreadsheets and business orientation. After five years, I began to search for a new beginning.

> Open the blinds: the first apricot blossoms have opened—Hurry! The spring days are now![4]
>
> —Cui Shaoxuan

Apricot and plum blossoms are a symbol for the awakening of mind after the stillness of concentration. As gardeners know, a cold winter is essential to the blossoming of fruit trees. In the same way, the stillness and clarity of mind through meditation gives birth to infinite creativity, which is our wild and precious life.

Through auspicious coincidence, I was introduced by a friend to Mountain Spirit Center, a new temple being built by a monk friend in the high desert of California. I dreamed of going there to practice and to serve this new community. After a brief conversation, it came into place.

The months living at Mountain Spirit Center renewed my great love affair with meditation practice. These months in the desert reconnected me with solitude. They gave me the opportunity to shed those layers of conditioning and roles that defined my socially constructed self. I needed to rediscover what was underneath those layers, to get reacquainted with my own ground of being. Having created vibrant, wide circles of connection, it was time to return to the stillness at their center. Through the gifts of solitude and intensive meditation practice, I had that opportunity to come home to myself. In addition to morning practice between 4:30 and 7 a.m., I chanted each day from nine to twelve.

CHANTING

While other Zen lineages have emphasized sitting Zen over chanting, Korean Zen has a strong and vibrant chanting tradition in addition to sitting Zen. When we are chanting, we give ourselves to this practice fully. Mind and body become one; inside and outside become one; we and our lives completely become one. At that moment, we attain our substance, which is a place before thinking. So we call this "don't-know mind." When you keep this mind one hundred percent, you are already the universe; the universe is you. You and everything already become one. We can call this experience Buddha nature, or God-nature, or the Tao; it exists before and beyond any name we can give to it. At this point we see clearly, hear clearly; everything is clear in front of us. The sky is blue; the grass is green. Then, how does this truth function to make our true, authentic, and moment-by-moment correct life?

When someone is hungry, give them food; if someone needs directions, show them which way to go. We may call that Great Love, Great Compassion, or in a Buddhist sense, the Great Bodhisattva Way—it is simply human nature, unobscured, clear and bright as the autumn moon in the night sky.

When we are chanting, we simply do it, one hundred percent. Within this practice, we become one with our substance: this is a direct experience of the ground of being. At this point, we and the world around us are not separate. Senses are purified, compassion arises, and we find our way. When we are chanting, we experience great energy as well as natural compassion; we can direct these towards a person or situation in need of healing. Korean people often do Kwan Seum Bosal *kidos* (chanting retreats) for this purpose.

Knowing I was doing a Kwan Seum Bosal hundred-day kido, many members of our community brought candles, fruit, and other gifts to the temple to support this practice. I was alone every morning and most of the day. In the desert, we had no cell signal, no T.V., no videos, no newspapers. The practice cleansed my field of perception so that I found myself connecting in a new way with the land itself, and through the land to all our relations.

Looking out the window at breakfast, I noticed the scent of sage and chaparral, and glimpsed baby mule deer, small and wobbly; lizards doing push-ups on our stairs; coyotes tracking across the property. Through seeing these animals, don't-know mind appeared. There is a beauty we recognize within the wild, within all nature. That same beauty is a part of us—we are also within nature. When we connect so completely with our life that we are one with our breath, one with our chant, one with our deepest prayer, we know this. The practice of living in right relationship to others and this world—when extended to animals, trees, and the environment—makes it possible for us to experience a deep intimacy, wisdom, and inner peace. These were the great gifts of this time— to recognize the presence of the land and to honor my relationship to the earth and all beings.

After six months of practice in the desert, I moved back into our circles of community, knowing that my calling is to work with people. Zen hermits always return to the marketplace. This place of practice, while challenging, offers the greatest opportunities to be of service, and thus, ultimately, the most spiritual growth. In Chinese tradition, a set of images called the Ten Ox-Herding Pictures evolved to describe the process of enlightenment. The last picture, titled *Returning Home with Open Hands*, shows Hotei, the "laughing Buddha," with a sack, symbolizing the treasure he has acquired: the light of clear mind. This treasure is our total experience: being right where we are. It is awakening to our life, this life. This is something we can experience right here and right now; in the midst of the storms that characterize this time of great change, we can find centeredness and peace. In these chapters that follow, we will journey through the four seasons, discovering Zen practice within the vividness of moment-by-moment life.

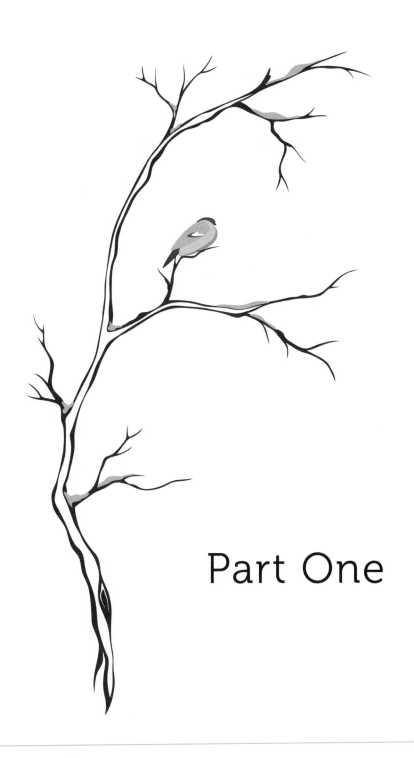

Part One

WINTER

Finding Light in the Darkness

In the deep quiet of winter, seeds are nourished within the dark earth. Within the winter landscape, pine, bamboo, and plum blossoms have traditionally been valued as symbols of perseverance and integrity. In the middle of winter, their fragrance nourishes us—and shows us that new life lies ahead.

Chapter 1

BRINGING FORTH THAT WHICH IS WITHIN

The wonderful thing about Zen practice is that everyone has the capacity to awaken. As Jakusho Kwong Roshi, a contemporary Zen master, says, "Whatever clarity, wisdom, insight we are looking for is already there. We just have to know it is there."[1]

Meditation practice is a practice of trusting our own eyes, ears, nose, tongue, body, mind—our own deepest experience. As we bring unconditional awareness to this moment, our mind and body become one; inside and outside become one; we and our life become one. We touch our ground of being, which in Zen tradition we call Buddha-nature. However, that place of stillness cannot be described in words. It is beyond any name we can give it. This still point is something we touch in moments of awe, when we look out at the Sierra Nevada Mountains or watch the stars at night. We also source from this still point when we are engaged in everyday activity—washing the dishes, folding laundry, making tea—and give ourselves to those actions with wholehearted attention. That experience of being awake to our life is our essence, our true nature. Practice is an act of trusting that essential nature and resting in that wholeness which we are. It is this intention to see the wholeness that then brings it forth in ourselves and others.

One element of this trust is developing an ability to rest the mind in the present moment. We are practicing being with ourselves as we are, and the moment just as it is. Woven into this is an element of letting go: letting go of our need to do something, our restlessness, our tendency to fill empty space with something—*anything*. We are nurturing calmness and self-acceptance. By creating this space within, our mind becomes clear like a mirror. This makes room for new ways of seeing and for the wisdom that is uniquely ours to emerge. In the Gospel of Thomas, there is a beautiful teaching attributed to Jesus:

> If you bring forth that which is within you, what is within you will save you. If you do not bring forth that which is within you, what is within you will destroy you.[2]

As we gain more confidence in our original nature, we are able to bring forth the insight and energy that is our treasure. This act of seeing the luminosity within is also the way that luminous awareness is cultivated. The seeds of wisdom and compassion awaken: we find our way.

Exercise: Centering

Placing your feet a shoulder's-width apart, stand in your natural, fully aligned posture, feeling your presence within the body. Breathe fully through the body: through the lungs and deeply through the lower abdomen. Place one hand three fingers below the navel, sensing the breath and its movement through the fingers of the hand. Let the out-breath be slightly longer than the in-breath, breathing in to a count of eight and breathing out to a count of ten.

Notice whether the breath is flowing freely or if it is constricted in any way. Where it is constricted, try to breathe through that. See if you can relax and soften that area as well. Rest in that awareness for a few minutes. Then place the hands palm-to-palm at heart level near the chest. Breathing in, bring these arms up above the head, taking a gentle stretch. Breathing out, bring the arms down in a big circle, as if you are embracing a huge orange or a beach ball, with fingers extended slightly. As the arms move, continue to keep awareness on the breath rising and falling in the lower abdomen. Let the movements of your arms follow the natural rhythms of your breath. Notice any physical sensations that arise. Notice that sense of wholeness that has arisen; know that you can connect to that at any time using the breath. This is the beginning of Zen practice.

Chapter 2

An Unbroken Circle, An Undivided Prayer

Interdependence is the true nature of our existence. This is not just an idea; it is physically true. All of the air we breathe has come through the forests; all of the earth's harvest comes to us through the work of many hands. All of our practice is training to recognize and trust the truth of our connection more than the illusion of separateness. This begins with recognizing the wholeness within ourselves—with our own ability to create space within and relax into this open space, with our ability to trust our experience just as it is. As we sit, many visitors will arrive at the gates of our awareness—thoughts, feelings, perceptions. Our practice is to let these visitors come and go without repressing them and without indulging them. Just as clouds come and go but the sky remains blue, our mind is not hindered by these visitors that come and go. When thoughts and feelings arise, we train in letting these be as they are. We are staying open to everything—pleasant and unpleasant feeling, the ecstasy and grief—without discarding or rejecting anything. Discovering this place of wholeness within, we have eyes to recognize this deep connection everywhere.

This practice of seeing with eyes of wholeness and connection is sourced from our body-centered awareness. We are rediscovering within our modern culture how essential it is to balance mind with heart and gut. More precisely, within the gut there is a place two inches below the navel called the *tandien* in Korean Zen, which serves as a reservoir of core strength. Tandien means "energy garden." Implicit in this designation is a strong value placed on body-centered and experiential knowing. In order for understanding to become wisdom, our mind must be well aligned with our heart and the power at our core. As my teacher Zen Master Seung Sahn would say, "Understanding is not enough. When you are doing something, just *do it*."

When we give ourselves to an activity one hundred percent, we experience the great power and energy that is available through being present. Within this experience of body/mind as a unified whole, and our ability to see with eyes of wholeness, there is a natural sense of ethics. Seeing how connected we are to everything in the universe, we naturally refrain from causing harm, as this would be causing harm to ourselves. In the beginning, this requires clear intention, but across time, we see this as a natural expression of our self, continuously coming into relation to the world.

This ethics of wholeness is profoundly needed right now. Within our society, our collective acquisition of knowledge currently outreaches our expression of wisdom. As Albert Einstein once said, "The release of atom power has changed everything except our way of thinking . . . the solution to this problem lies in the heart of mankind."[1] The technological advances of this century have given us greater mastery of the physical world without requisite co-development of the heart. Thus, as a species we have resistance to our own unfolding at this critical time. In order to take the next steps together to make a future possible for our children, we need to re-awaken our inner compass by connecting with that hidden wholeness, our awakened heart/mind, and take action that reconnects whole communities. In order to live well, it is necessary to come into alignment with family, community, the natural world—discerning and honoring all our relations. We then find ourselves within a sacred and undivided circle.

This undivided circle is represented within Tibetan Buddhist tradition by the *mandala*. A mandala is a traditional geometric design, often circular. Carl Jung succinctly described the purpose of the mandala:

Within the mandala there is a central point or focus within the symbol from which radiates a symmetrical design. This suggests there is a center within each one of us to which everything is related, by which everything is ordered, and which is itself a source of energy and power.[2]

A mandala simultaneously represents an inner landscape and the physical realm within which every element of experience is unified, balanced, and complete. In Tibetan tradition, to see a mandala is considered a great blessing, as it conveys a deep impression of wholeness, bringing about healing and peace. Mandalas can be created with varied materials, including grain, precious metal, and flowers. The most intricate and beautiful mandalas have been made with particles of colored sand. Each element of the sand mandala has precise symbolic meaning. In the Tibetan practice of the sand mandala, psychodynamic energies are represented through five colors, each one containing the potential for expression in either its static or dynamic, awakened form.[3]

The color blue represents the sharp piercing blue of the spring sky; this lucidity and clarity can manifest as anger or as the sword that cuts through delusion. The color yellow represents the golden energy of increase: fertility, prosperity, abundance; this energy can give rise to pride. At the moment we truly apprehend the blessings always pouring forth, it becomes a sense of natural appreciation and generosity. Red represents the attachment of passion. Through luminous awareness, the red thread of passion opens the door to compassion: we see that others are also rendered vulnerable by their pursuit of happiness. Like the lotus that arises out of muddy water, we discover a way of enjoying the world without grasping tightly onto anything. Free from grasping, "enough mind" naturally magnetizes to itself all that is beneficial. The color green, when operating in a static form, arises as competitiveness and jealousy. When we open to awareness without reference point, we are free from the illusion of scarcity. Free from fear, one can see the resources at hand and thus take action. This energy becomes the wisdom that accomplishes and completes all things.

At the center of the mandala, the color is white: the ego defense that is cured at this point is the root error of ignorance, the mental confusion that brings about our other misperceptions. When one sees past the illusion of separation to the truth of our interdependence with each other and this world, the seeds of anger, attachment, and fear have no place to take root. In a dynamic sense, the white color represents the illumination of complete realization.

The geometric structures portrayed within the mandala are the structures of human consciousness. The surrounding circle represents dynamic awareness. The square symbolizes the four directions, the physical world. At each side of the square, a gate is constructed. These represent the four immeasurables: loving-kindness, compassion, sympathetic joy, and equanimity; through these practices one enters sacred ground.

Of all these exquisite gifts of beauty, the greatest teaching of the sand mandala is actually within its dismantling ceremony. Upon completion of the sand mandala, there is a powerful ceremony that celebrates its completion and recognizes its impermanence. The mandala design is cut with the point of a *vajra*, or as it is known in the Tibetan language, a *dorje*: a ritual instrument symbolizing the indestructible nature of pure consciousness. The word *dorje* translates as "king of stones." Pure consciousness is diamond-like in its brilliance and adamantine quality.[4] The light of awakening cuts through illusion. In this case, the dorje cuts through the mandala so that we see clearly— this mandala form, so intricate and precious, is like the human body, also of the nature of impermanence.

It is significant, too, that the ceremony does not end with the sweeping up of sand. The sand is not a static ingredient. By some Tibetan translations, the Tibetan word for mandala, *dkyil 'khor*, means "to extract the essence."[5] With any sand mandala, the essence being extracted is the essence of earth. This extraction is not done with the intent of using or exploiting this essence; "extracting the essence" refers to a process of accomplishing, and lifting up to awareness, the essence of earth. Having received so much life force from the earth, the mandala raises this to awareness as a gift of beauty and harmony. So it is with all sand mandala offerings that upon completion the sand is ceremonially gathered and taken to a body of water through which it is offered to the water and all beings within it. The reciprocal relationship between earth and the practitioners is thus brought into perfect alignment.

The gift of the mandala is in its power to transform our own minds and the environment around us into a celestial realm, awakening us to the sacred aspect of earth, our inseparable connection to all people and other forms of life.

Our life is a mandala, unfolding before us. As we come into relationship with others and this world, bringing each situation into balance, this creates a pattern of harmony and beauty around us. The emotions of passion, aversion, even fear—when fully met with unconditional presence—are transformed into their jewel-like essence. Every person that enters our life is bringing us exactly what we need to complete the circle.

When I lead meditation, I set the cushions in the shape of a circle so that we can benefit from the tangible experience of the ways in which we are all in this together. Our collective dynamic awareness is the foundation of our meditation session. Whoever enters the circle is exactly who needs to be there. Each visitor bears a gift for our collective awakening. We are breathing together, each breath a tidal rhythm that connects us to the whole. Each person's presence and clarity affects the entire circle.

This can be described scientifically using neuropsychology through the paradigm of *resonance:* body/mind systems attune to other body/minds. There is also a natural process of attunement. When we drop into our body-centered awareness and attend to another from this place of deep listening and wholeness, it has a healing effect upon the other, which ripples out into their relationships. When one person practices empathy, it is scientifically proven that people three degrees away begin to become kinder. This awareness of the unbroken circle is also powerfully expressed in traditional wisdom teachings, practices, and ceremonies. In many indigenous practices, this mandala is expressed as a circle that includes all living beings and this natural world. This powerful sense of connection to all our relations is also found within Korean Zen teaching. My teacher Zen Master Seung Sahn often said, "If you have a question, ask a tree. The tree will give you a good answer." All the natural world presses us to come more fully into our own experience: mind and body becoming one, inside and outside becoming one. Our own inner universe—earth, water, air, and the fire of life—reflects the sacred earth; the wholeness of our body rhythms reflects the interconnectedness of natural rhythms, the dynamic change we witness as tides rise and fall. In receiving teaching from tides and this great earth, we find our innate wholeness, the mandala that is our life.

This unbroken circle encompasses the full spectrum of our moment-to-moment experience; to be able to feel and be present to joy, we also need to feel and be present to pain. Sometimes when doing ceremony for people, the healing gift that Carl Big Heart, a spiritual teacher, brings is that he is able to cry with them; he is not turning away. In Carl's words,

> We carry the pain of our ancestors. We need to be open to the shared grief of each other. To be open to feel this consciously, to consciously choose, and to do this work: this is what heals.

This is the path of the Bodhisattva: one breath, one undivided circle.

EXERCISE: SITTING ZEN

Connect with the rhythms of breath using the Centering exercise. Now find a seat. A firm cushion is ideal. Sitting cross-legged or in a kneeling position on the floor is optimal; a chair will also work. If sitting on a cushion cross-legged, try to bring your knees into contact with the ground. Let the shoulders be back so that the lungs and heart can be open. The hands can be placed in a traditional *mudra* (posture), forming an oval with the fingers of the left over the fingers of the right, thumbs touching, against the abdomen at the tandien, three fingers below the navel. Let the eyes focus softly, resting at a thirty-degree angle to the floor.

For an inner technique, bring awareness to the rhythms of breath as you can sense them at the tandien. Let the out-breath be slightly longer than the in-breath. As a touchstone, you can count the breath up to ten and then begin again or use a repetitive phrase, for instance *clear mind, clear mind, clear mind* on the in-breath, *don't know* on the out-breath. *Clear mind* is simply a reminder to us to drop the storyline and be with what *is*. *Don't know* is our mind before thinking, that luminous awareness that is our true nature. As the mind wanders, gently bring it back to the breath and to the moment. This is traditional Zen practice, Sitting Zen.

As you sit, notice any physical sensations that arise within this. Notice where the in-breath ends and the out-breath begins. As the mind wanders, continue to notice it and bring the mind back. Notice any physical patterns of constriction or expansion that surface, as well as any emotional or cognitive patterns. Continue to stay with the direct experience of these as a felt sense. Ask yourself, "What is going on for me right now, and can I be with it, completely?" Try this for ten minutes.

Chapter 3

HOPE

On a certain autumn afternoon in Boston, the energy is dramatically changing. Daylight saving time having taken effect, sunset is 4:30 p.m. With the weather having abruptly dropped twenty degrees, we've arrived overnight at the cusp of winter. Changes in our environment are mirrored by changes in the energy of our collective psyche. The abruptness of the energy shift raises the contrast and lifts this energy to awareness. Outside with some students, I receive the most sincere questions I've ever received about practice, sincere in the sense that their comments risked something and revealed something.

Some people wonder whether spiritual practice is effective . . .
Some people question whether nonviolent tactics are naïve . . .
I read a book that critiqued the Dalai Lama . . .

The questions reflect back the students' minds—and their sense of grief and pain as well as their concern for finding something that is truly authentic, some way to get at the root. I shared with them the calligraphy at a Chinese temple door that has stayed with me:

> Ten thousand gold pieces turn to dust in one day
> One moment of looking into the self, thousand-year treasure.[1]

I told stories of Cambodia and India, the immense power of nonviolence, and the experience in Chicago of nonviolence as a powerful movement. I spoke of the absolute necessity of positive collective social action for a future to be possible.

The intergovernmental reports on climate change clearly confirm this. No single country, and certainly no single administration, can make the immense, wide-ranging changes in emissions and sustainable energy that our earth requires. This can and will happen as communities work together as agents of change. The first steps towards change are very grassroots: we need to transform the causes and conditions within us and find more people to share our vision with. We draw inspiration and support from each other. Within practice, this process of connecting with our shadow, and its invitation of despair, is very valuable. Through this practice faith arises, which is based on experience. As Rumi writes:

> Don't turn your head. Keep looking
> at the bandaged place.
> That's where the light enters.[2]

Through the courage that penetrates into our own dark night, we can transmute and receive the gifts of the shadow—and these dark nights become the source of medicine to heal our world. We need to consciously train in hope, nourish our spirits, become the change we seek, and find people to share our vision. As we do this, we discover the inner resources of clarity, compassion, and insight that have always been with us. Just as seeds that have been dormant for a thousand years—when watered and cared for—produce beautiful flowers, our awakened heart/mind, the seed of our true nature, is within us. The practices offered throughout this book will provide rich soil for its blossoming.

Exercise: Feed Your Spirit

Take a moment to reflect on what you love, what opens your heart. What is it that reconnects you with your sense of hope and the infinite ways that the universe is supporting us? Take some time and look at the stars, stroll through a garden, read a book of poetry, bake a loaf of bread, raise your voice in song. That experience of beauty feeds our spirits and makes it possible for us to be a source of hope and beauty for the world.

DIALOGUE

My students ask many beautiful questions. I include some of these here, as you may also have these questions.

In order to practice Zen, is it necessary to consider oneself Buddhist?

No, it is not. In fact, it may be easier to practice Zen without previous experience. Our goal in Zen is to keep "don't-know mind," that mind that is open to everything just as it is. Many people practicing Zen meditation identify themselves as Christian, Jewish, Muslim, Unitarian Universalist, or from other wisdom traditions. They find that Buddhist meditation increases their self-insight and compassion.

Zen is a practice rather than a belief system. This can actually be very liberating. Recognizing this as a practice, we don't have to have it all together the first time we sit down to meditate. In fact, noticing when our mind wanders is as much a part of meditation as the moments of focus. When we bring unconditional awareness to our restlessness or our perfectionism, these obstacles themselves become the path, bearing rich gifts. By taking a nonjudgmental attitude towards whatever arises, we create space within for our deepest growth.

What is the optimal amount of time to sit meditation?

The best amount of time to sit meditation depends on your own intention and commitment. What amount of time can you commit to every day and show up for consistently without putting undue pressure on yourself? Meditation practice is like gardening: we tend the garden every day, and across time this consistency produces an effect. It is usually helpful to designate the same time each day, so that you find a natural rhythm.

Why do things happen?

This is a common question my students have asked, concerning the challenges that arise in life and which may seem unmerited, capricious, and unjust. His Holiness the Dalai Lama answered this beautifully at a recent teaching in Boston:

> First, for a Buddhist, we can believe that, given the continuity of energy from a past life, this is completing a cycle. If we are nonreactive, this pattern loses its momentum and the balance of our life energy shifts towards more favorable conditions.

Second, for a secular person, it is helpful to consider how things are interrelated. Taking a hawk's-eye perspective, we can see the same situation with different approaches from different angles. Even in a challenging situation, there may be the potential for growth and new opportunities. We can see that a tragedy happened through various causes and conditions, past conditions and present conditions. In this way, we are able to be more objective; through this realistic approach, we can see another, more positive side to each situation. Everything has the potential for good, or goodness; everything is workable. Sometimes the chaos we encounter offers the best opportunities for our soul's growth. And we should inquire closely into our approaches to happiness.

Some of the ways we have of seeking happiness—through money, pharmaceuticals, possessions, fame, among others—are not so effective. True happiness comes from inner peace, based on contentment and genuine love and compassion. This is something that we can actually experience through meditation. [3]

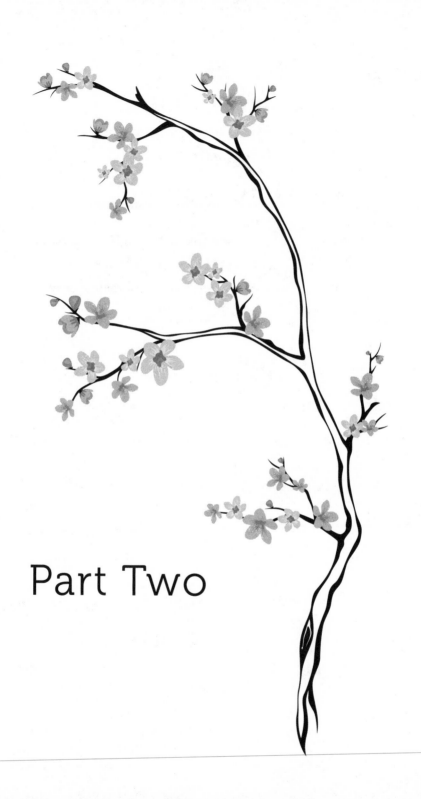

Part Two

Spring

New Life
Beginning

Seeds planted in fertile soil break through the ground,
nourished by sun and soft spring rains. These new beginnings take courage—and bring forth the greatest beauty.

Chapter 4

THE LION'S ROAR

As I've mentioned, these are times of great change, which present great opportunity to awaken as well as intensify experience of our patterns of holding and contraction. The Lion's Roar is the charge we are given as a way to meet the energies within and the energies of this time. This teaching is described in the Lotus Sutra as a response to the Vedic prophecy of the Kali Yuga. The Lion's Roar is actually a great vow of compassion, which arises out of complete openness and transparency.

This teaching is shown in Ashokan (ancient Indian) art as four lions facing the four directions. As we move toward our life experience, not holding back anything, we have access to the highest energy, complete fearlessness.[1] We find the courage to take off our armor, and our golden lion nature is revealed. Moment by moment, this openness becomes a raw new place to live from, and our light moves others to awaken.

Through our practice of staying open, staying connected to our intentions of compassion, our practices of seeing how we are not separate from anything in the universe, we live our way into an enlightened world. Our energy radiates through to others. Every action, every thought, is like a stone thrown into water, rippling in widening circles. And this is creating our world. This can start in quite a simple way: through being present with our own body/mind, unconditionally. Within mindfulness practice, we bring awareness fully into present time through watching the breath or working with other touchstones that anchor our awareness in this moment.

As you are reading this, you could try this now. Centering yourself in your body, notice the sensation of the breath, this river of life that is moving through you. Bring awareness to the breath in the lower abdomen, the lungs, the nostrils—wherever it is most clearly perceptible to you. Notice any physical sensations that accompany this awareness—sensations of warmth or coolness, sensations of pressure or tingling—any sensations at all.

Notice, as well, any thoughts or emotional content that arise. Let this be as it is.

Without repressing and without identifying with these patterns, we simply let it all move through. As we sit, the body/mind releases energy. We may experience this release as a blessing, as bliss. We may experience the release as edginess, itchiness. In a way, these are two sides of the same phenomenon. These energies are inner weather patterns. They are like the elements: earth, air, fire, water.

We can experience great energy, even a kind of joy, in letting these weather patterns simply move through. The space between exhilaration and fear, between anxiety and bliss, is as close as a single breath.

Our renewed connection with the body requires that we accept everything in our body/mind unconditionally. There is not even "body" and "mind," simply one whole *bodymind*. This *is* the work. As we open to accept our experience, the act of observing our experience already shifts it. This is the alchemy of meditation practice: transmuting poison into medicine. Opening to restlessness, we may discover it is actually some energy we have swept into the closet, perhaps resentment or insecurity. Opening to anger unconditionally, it heightens. We can experience this like the lava of a volcano—pure energy: heat, fire, movement—and simply let it go.

Bringing unconditional awareness and deep listening to our experience of anger, dropping the storyline and being with this energy unconditionally, we will notice that it shifts. We may see that pattern and energy as a more primary experience of grief or pain. Again, practicing being with our experience wholeheartedly, we listen and attend—noticing where this sensation may be experienced within our body and breathing through it. This requires *kshanti*, patience. Within Buddhist traditions, patience is described in an active sense, as forbearance: active *bearing with*.

The practice of the Lion's Roar is radical vulnerability, staying in this open, uncertain space—not resisting, not denying, not holding back. In Katagiri Roshi's words, "We forgive the entire universe for being itself."[2] We are willing to dance in the fire, not holding back anything. When it rains, we are soaked to the bone. That willingness begins to unravel pain and discomfort—but to what degree, or at what time? This is a matter of divine timing, and so it is that this practice is easier said than done. Given time, this pain transmutes into the tenderness of compassion. Opening to our own pain unconditionally, we discover the gifts of self-empathy and sensitivity, as well as our capacity for love.

The Lion's Roar is thus the core practice, and our charge for these challenging times. Whether the obstacles are experienced as inner demons or collectively, at this time of kairos, the instructions are the same.

EXERCISE: MINDFULNESS OF THE BODY

Connect with the rhythms of breath using the Centering exercise. Begin Sitting Zen, bringing awareness to the rhythms of breath as you can sense them at the tandien. Count the breaths or use a repetitive phrase, for instance *clear mind, clear mind, clear mind, don't know.* As the mind wanders, gently bring it back to the breath and to the moment. As you sit, notice any physical patterns of constriction or expansion that surface: notice any pulse, pressure, or tingling. See if you can notice where the in-breath ends and the out-breath begins. Notice if the breath is flowing freely or if it is constricted in any area. Where there is a pattern of constriction, see if you can breathe through this and relax and soften this area of the body. Notice how the emotions associated with this area also begin to shift. Perhaps these emotions, which seem so solid, are actually interweaving patterns of energy. When we make contact with these patterns through the breath, we free up stored energy for our own becoming. Try this for fifteen minutes.

Chapter 5

EMPATHY

The practice of mindfulness we've just completed creates the foundation for empathy. Having extended this compassion and deep listening to ourselves, we are now able to extend compassion and deep listening to the people and situations we encounter. When we extend this deep listening to ourselves and others, we touch a place of wholeness, clarity, and well-being. It makes it possible for the other person to sense their own inherent worth and tap into their own inner resources.

This learning how to extend kindness originates with our first, most essential relationship: that of a mother with her child. Just as a mother may optimally extend unconditional presence to her child, so we aspire to be present with all beings. The Metta Sutra, one of the earliest Buddhist texts, expresses loving-kindness in just this way:

> May all beings be happy
> May they be joyous and live in safety

All living beings whether weak or strong

In high or middle or low realms of existence

Small or great visible or invisible near or far born
  or to be born

May all beings be happy

Let no one deceive another nor despise any being
  in any state

Let none by anger or hatred wish harm to another

Even as a mother at the risk of her life

Watches over and protects her only child

So with a boundless mind should one cherish all
  living things

Suffusing love over the entire world

Above below and all around without limit

So let one cultivate an infinite good will toward
  the entire world

Standing walking sitting or lying down

During all one's waking hours

Let one practice the way with gratitude

Not holding to fixed views

Endowed with insight

One who achieves the way
  will be freed from the duality of birth and
  death[1]

Let's reflect upon the first two lines: May all beings be happy. May all beings be joyous and live in safety.

The point of spiritual practice is to understand our self and to be of service, to help others. Just as I want to be happy, all beings want to be happy. As Mother Teresa once said, "The problem with the world is that we draw the circle of our family too small." By opening our heart in this widened circle, we are mending the separateness that creates suffering and conflict and creating peace.

This practice truly does ripple out to all our relations. The Omega Institute, where I teach over the summer, offers programs drawn from a very diverse range of wisdom traditions to support the awakening of the spirit. It is located on an idyllic campus in the Hudson River Valley. The animals there have gained an extraordinary level of trust and familiarity with human ways. Skunks root for dinner on the front lawn; cottontails romp near the trapeze platforms. In one vivid and recent experience during the process of writing this book, as I sat in the main garden, a groundhog drew near and then placed his paws upon my legs in the manner of a dog requesting attention. One morning, a tiny hummingbird with its sudden, brilliant movements approached a seated merlin falcon, curious and playful, and then whirred down to the sanctuary pond to drink from the golden flowers at the water's edge. This level of ease and trust arises out of the practice of kindness.

Exercise: Metta Practice

Connect with luminous awareness using the Sitting Zen. Resting in awareness, repeat these phrases silently to yourself over the span of five to fifteen minutes:

> May I be filled with loving-kindness; may I be held
>   in loving-kindness.
> May I accept myself just as I am.
> May I experience the innate joy of being alive.
> May my heart and mind awaken.
> May I be free.[2]

Allow yourself to fully receive this gift of self-love. Trust this loving-kindness more than any self-limiting thought. Rest in this quality of self-empathy, continuing to extend this unconditional kindness to whatever arises in the heart/mind.

Now, envisioning someone you have an unconditional positive regard for, someone for whom you find it very easy to feel unconditional love—a close friend, grandmother, anyone at all—generate loving-kindness once again:

> May you be filled with loving-kindness;
> May you be held in loving-kindness.
> May you accept yourself just as you are.

May you experience the innate joy of being alive.
May your heart and mind awaken; may you be free.

As you generate loving-kindness for this person, envision them in the full light of their original nature: radiant, vitally present, and whole. Let other thoughts or conditions drop away. See the beauty and grace of their spirit. Rest in this unconditional kindness for five to fifteen minutes.

Now, envisioning all the people within your family, the people of your community, people in this country, and people in other countries—birds in the air, fish in the water, and all the creatures that share this earth with us—widen the circle again.

May all beings be filled with loving-kindness.
May all beings have deep and lasting peace.
May all beings experience the innate joy of being
alive.
May all beings awaken; may they all be free.

As you generate loving-kindness, begin with the people and communities that come easily to mind. From there, extend loving-kindness to other countries, all beings, this natural world. *Just as we want to be happy, all beings want to be happy.* Feel and trust the truth of that connection. Rest in this loving-kindness for five to fifteen minutes. (Thank you to Vipassana teacher Tara Brach for these lovely phrases.)

Chapter 6
SPRING CLEANING— TRAVELING LIGHTLY

In some ways, it feels natural to me to travel lightly, having been a nun for fifteen years, living in a Zen center, interweaving this with ninety-day retreats that usually included a preparatory move of all belongings into storage. Now, living on my own, I still travel and teach for three months of the year. All of this requires simplifying, periodically giving away clothes, books, anything that can be released. Mostly, I find it easy.

At the same time, change is unsettling—and so, the process of picking up everything and moving has been deeply disturbing at times. To open this door, other doors close for the moment. And the longing for home presses upon me like an insistent cat.

As a young Zen student, I often watched my teacher Dae Bong Sunim pack for teaching trips, a model of monastic simplicity and Virgoan order. For a week of retreat:

five pairs of socks, five t-shirts, two sweaters, formal robes, electric razor, and essential toiletries, all neatly stacked inside a gray backpack. In my own packing, I strive for that level of order and simplicity, letting the packing for a trip itself be a reflection of clear mind, enough mind. Intentional simplicity is one way of practicing as a monk: letting what we have be enough. Fittingly enough, in packing for a recent trip, I found a copy of the forty-nine-day funeral ceremony: the ultimate sorting-out process.

In Buddhist tradition, we believe that our current path continues after this life through a natural law of conservation of energy. This perspective may help one to discern a deeper purpose in the circumstances of life—seeing both gifts and challenges as part of a journey of awakening. The continuation of our path in the afterlife is considered a refining process, which is estimated to take forty-nine days. For this reason, the forty-nine-day funeral ceremony is considered especially significant.

In Korean Zen, the path after life is mythically described as a visit to the place of the Ten Kings. For forty-nine days, the Ten Kings weigh out the result of one's actions and decide what kind of rebirth the person will then receive. However, the true meaning of this time is that upon death our consciousness expands; our entire life comes before us, and we are drawn to complete the lessons that comprise the next step of our evolutionary journey. If there are deep *samskara*, patterns of anger, anxiety, or other cognitive-emotional attachments, these may continue to set our agenda. If there are affinities based on clarity and kindness, these also may accompany us. The Ten Kings are created by our mind. Ultimately, we can't fool our true self. There are many things about that point beyond death that are, from a Zen perspective, beyond our ken. However, if we want to understand that future point, we can look closely at the present moment: the present moment gives birth to the future. By living in alignment with the world around us and doing our spiritual work with ongoing attentiveness, we can die in alignment and at peace with ourselves.

As I prepare for this trip, I have been sorting-out in this wider way. Reconciliation with a colleague helps me have less extra baggage. Attending my fifteen-year college reunion helped me let go of old ghosts. These reconciliations, this dropping of the old story, is the ultimate traveling light. I have learned the most powerful lessons on forgiveness from those who have the most to forgive. Steven Charleston, a Native American Episcopal Bishop, is one of these who has shared powerful words:

> Reconciliation is not about forgiving or forgetting. It is not possible to forget the stories of our people. Forgiving is something that comes over time; it is a gift to the one who forgives. Reconciliation carries the energetic sense of offering an amnesty, based on our

shared humanity. It involves being willing to live in the same house and disagree. This involves vulnerability and being comfortable with there not being one way[1] [what in Zen we would call not-knowing].

In this description, Bishop Charleston called upon images from the Bible, particularly the countless stories of Jesus doing things the incorrect way: performing healings on the wrong day, with the wrong people. Also dressing the wrong way. So perhaps the Christian savior is not one who is so concerned that things be done right. And there are countless stories where Jesus sees his disciples disagree. In Zen tradition, we have this, too. Buddhist sutras contain hundreds of stories of the Buddha mediating disputes within the monastic Sangha. So perhaps Jesus and Buddha expected their disciples to disagree. The wonder—the miracle—is to find a way to disagree and share the same table. To quote the Dhammapada, one of the earliest Buddhist texts:

> There are those who know we are always facing death.
> Knowing this, they put aside all quarrels.[2]

There is some homework within this for all of us. Where in your life can you take a step towards forgiveness; where can you offer an amnesty?

Of course, throughout our lives we will be challenged to develop relationships that honor ourselves and others in equal balance. We will be called to discern the delicate balance between keeping the peace and true peacemaking. This will require a tolerance for differences, even those differences that run most deep, as well as healthy boundaries—through which true connection is possible, through which a balance is found between giving and receiving. This is our shared koan as our world continues to become more interconnected, while climate change and other dilemmas require collaborative solutions.

The path of awakening is a continual stripping away and releasing. This practice of letting go is exemplified by the Tibetan monks and nuns who create the sand mandalas described in chapter 2. They bring deep devotion and meticulousness to each grain of sand in the creation of these infinite and beautiful mandalas and then dismantle the mandala as soon as it is completed.

I have had the great honor of seeing this process up close through the nuns of Keydong Thuk-Che-Cho-Ling Nunnery in Kathmandu. These nuns, the first ever trained in this art traditionally reserved for monks, created a mandala of Avalokitesvara, the archetype of compassion, at Wellesley College. The Keydong nuns were great Dharma friends and teachers in their ability to travel lightly. They traveled here from Kathmandu with the simplest of possessions—just robes and colored sand—

sharing the weight of their maroon-clothed parcels quite cheerfully together. They adapted to our culture and situation with resilience and playfulness. The next day, they began creating a mandala of Avalokitesvara grain by grain with exquisite attentiveness, precision, and joy. And with equal joy, they returned the sand to the lake at the mandala's completion.

Just before I left for a sabbatical in California, Ani Tendol, the leader of the Keydong nuns, again visited, and we shared breakfast, gazing at the bridge where the ceremony of returning the sand was held. As we sat there, I could sense in a new way, as if for the first time, how letting go creates space for new joy to enter. Just as the sun rises and sets, there is a deep peace in being part of all of this. As I allowed myself to sense this natural peace, I discovered that the sanctuary that I craved was already within me. Like the turtle, which carries its home on its back, each step of the journey could be experienced as a true home in the present moment.

EXERCISE: CLEAN HOUSE

Make a list of what needs to be released in your life in order to make room for new beginnings; physically, this may include crates of storage in the basement or clothes that you never wear. Donate it all to a worthy cause. On the emotional level, whom do you need to forgive?

Whom do you need to ask forgiveness of? If this were your last day on Earth, what unfinished business would you clear up? No one guarantees your life. All of us have only moments to live. Find those people and have those conversations today. Mentally, what self-limiting beliefs need to be released? When sitting meditation, what familiar storylines arise, what scripts arise in your life with too-familiar roles of hero or victim, parent, child, teacher? Throw them all away. Write these down on a piece of paper; burn it using a fireproof container, setting the intention to release whatever needs to be released in order to make room for new beginnings.

When we create new, clear space for our life, it is essential to have a clear compass—a way of discerning, among all these possibilities, which is most aligned with our spirit. Very often, students come to my office asking questions about their relationship to the world. Should they take this major because it is fun, or this major that is considered marketable? Should they follow a pre-med track to fulfill their parents' expectations, or study art history? Is this relationship the right one—and what does Buddhism say about relationships? The answer to these questions is simple—and challenging.

The Buddha set up ethical guidelines for clear living, which are called the precepts. The precepts help us to find happiness by describing simple ways we can avoid causing harm to others. The first five precepts are found within all wisdom traditions: they set intentions not to take life, steal, lie, or abuse alcohol or sexuality. Life presents us with many different situations; very often, we already instinctively know what the right thing to say or do is. However, when weather conditions are a bit overcast and we cannot see our way through, the precepts help us to find our way.

In Buddhist tradition, there is an ancient design that reflects this process of discernment; it is based on the North Star. Many world cultures have used the North Star for navigation because it points the way unerringly. We navigate by the North Star by aligning with these simple guidelines for clear action, which are the precepts. However, in Zen practice, we ultimately find that North Star within ourselves. Zen Master Seung Sahn often asked his students, "What is the most important thing?" He compared Zen practice to the business of real estate, in which it is all about "location, location, location." Just in that way, our Zen practice can be described very simply as "direction, direction, direction." Why do you do what you do? For whom? If our actions are only for ourselves, they will at some point run aground; they will not be sustainable, so far as they are not truly aligned with the laws of existence. Whereas, if we take action based on a direction of compassion and being of service, these life directions will bring us more expediently and gracefully within the flow of energy that is creation.

Exercise: Setting Our Course

In Zen centers, we begin each morning with a vow to be of service and help others. In other forms of Buddhist practice, there are beautiful prayers of dedication in which the benefit we may receive from positive actions is dedicated to others. Find a way in which your own aspiration to awaken and be of service can be expressed in words that are meaningful to you. For instance, one of my own vows is "to aspire to see the beauty and wholeness within each person I make contact with today." Let this vow take a shape that is heartfelt and true for you—and that aligns with the direction of your life.

Chapter 7

INDRA'S NET—SEE THE CONNECTIONS

In Zen, one image we use to describe our interdependence with each other is Indra's Net. In Hindu tradition, Indra is the king of the gods; the common use of this image within Buddhism is symbolic rather than religious, yet it reveals the deep kinship between these traditions. Imagine a net: the horizontal threads representing time, the vertical threads representing space. At the point where each of these threads meet, there is a crystal that is reflecting not only every other crystal, but also every reflection of every other crystal. Just in this way, we are always coming into being together. We are composed of these reflections of each other. These deep connections are the truth of our existence.

For instance, this book that rests in your hands is interdependent with the trees, which gave the paper that forms these pages. It is interdependent with the teachers who have entered my life, with the students in whose presence these stories came to life across many years. It is interdependent with our collective experience of huge societal change that spurred me to write as a way of offering healing that can bring about peace, breath by breath. Within a single page of paper, we see our relatedness and deep connection with everything in the universe like roots running deep underground.

This understanding was vividly brought home to me on one ordinary day. On that particular day, I had a clear sense of making connections, which was entirely about logistics driven by a tight schedule. Waking at 5:05 a.m., practicing meditation until 6:25 a.m., leaving the house to catch the 7 a.m. bus from Kendall Square, Cambridge, to Wellesley College. Arriving at 8 a.m. at Wellesley, making Xeroxes and delivering them to student government for a noon event, making Xeroxes for my stress-reduction class, catching the 9 a.m. bus—and arriving in Kendall Square at 10 a.m., right on schedule. Now I was right where I needed to be to catch the subway downtown for a stress-reduction class I teach at lunchtime in the Financial District.

This is where the universe provides a new lesson.

As I get out of the subway train, I momentarily look down, adjusting the two bags I am carrying and the box of Xeroxes, rebalancing. In that moment, I hear something, a brief chorus of sound. As I look up, I see someone has fallen backward on the escalator. The man is, in fact, still falling head first; his head bumps each steel step. With each lurch downward, my stomach jumps. This moment seems expanded, as if time has stopped. His falling down the "up" escalator seems to defy laws of gravity.

At that moment, for a moment, I pause. There is a man farther up the escalator near the falling man's out-stretched legs who is stopping his fall by grabbing his leg. To my side, there are a bevy of passers-by who have decided it is a good day to take the elevator, the door of which is closing. In that moment, the illusion of a neatly constructed agenda hovers—and disappears. This is the connection I need to make: extending a hand, however awkward it could feel. Even as I run up the escalator, a part of my mind still cries out, "What can you do? You are not built brawnily enough to haul this man back on his feet." Yet, as I get there, the second man on the escala-tor is struggling to pull him to his feet, or at least away from the teeth of the escalator. I lean and push from be-hind; as the man's form caves backward, I see a place to give a focused push, the kind learned in volleyball. The second man catches his body, anchors it forward, and the man finds his feet. Just at that moment, we arrive at the top of the escalator. I check in with him. "Are you okay?" He replies that he is. A woman says, "You hit your head." He replies, "That's okay, I don't keep much in it." He was, no doubt, ready for a chiropractic appointment the next day, but no other injury occurred.

Someone, later that day, expressed surprise that I had not stopped to consider the bags I'd left at the bottom of the escalator. I know that for me, the bags were not in the way of a spontaneous response. Meditation practice helps me step out of my own way, to see the connection, and to respond. Every now and then, I do get a wake-up call, and although the experiences initially are gut wrenching, at the end I feel more alive and more authentic, more myself. So, did I help him, or did I help myself?

Is there a difference?

KUAN YIN/KWAN SEUM BOSAL

The archetype of Kwan Seum Bosal illuminates this point: that wherever we find ourselves, we are deeply connected to others and this world. Kwan Seum Bosal is the Korean name for the Bodhisattva of compassion. Kwan Seum Bosal is an archetype, based on the historical Avalokitesvara, a disciple of the Buddha who, in deep meditation, perceives the sound of the world, and with that sound, the pain that all beings experience. At that moment, the disciple recognizes he is not separate from it and makes a great vow of compassion to help all beings. Kwan Seum Bosal thus represents the compassion within us as well as the compassion all around us. Perceiving clearly, we see we have our work clear in front of us. At the same time, seeing and trusting the truth of our connection, we can source from this universal energy. As a koan asks, "Kwan Seum Bosal has ten thousand hands and eyes. Which are the correct hands and eyes?" Right now, as we allow ourselves to become one with the awakened energy of compassion, we discover all the power we need.

There is a story my friend Nawang Khechog tells of a French monk studying in Dharmsala, using the Guide to the Bodhisattva's Way of Life as a reference. The Guide to the Bodhisattva's Way of Life is a practice of compassion and loving-kindness. During the monk's studies, he became distracted by a beautiful nun. Finally, the monk could take it no longer. He went to His Holiness the Dalai Lama and begged to be relieved from the loving-kindness practice that was making him more susceptible to the charms of the nun. The Dalai Lama replied, "Even if you were to break the most serious precepts of the monastic code a hundred times, even if you were to break the auxiliary precepts a thousand times, still you should not stop practicing loving-kindness!"[1]

That is how deeply compassion is woven into the root of our practice.

EXERCISE: BEING TREES

When we see a grove of aspen, they appear to be separate trees. Actually, they are one tree, connected at the root; one source nourishes the entire grove. We recognize that presence and beauty we see within the forest because we also are that. We are nature. This exercise is an expression of our deep connection with the elements, and with all beings.

We begin with the same position we used for the Centering exercise in chapter 1. With your feet a shoulder's-width apart, stand in your natural, fully aligned posture, feeling your presence within the body. Envision yourself as a great tree. Breathe fully through the body: through the lungs and deeply through the lower abdomen. Breathe through the soles of the feet. Envision roots going deep through your breath into the earth. As you do so, sense yourself nourished by your friends, families, communities, the natural world—everything that grounds and nourishes you at your root. Now, place the hands palm-to-palm at heart level near the chest. Breathing in, bring these arms up above the head, taking a gentle stretch. Reaching up with our arms, we connect with that clear light that is our true nature, letting it nourish every cell in our body. Take a moment to rest in this healing awareness. Breathing out, now bring the arms to heart level, letting these two energies of rootedness and clear light come together and bring joy to us.

EXERCISE: MANTRA PRACTICE

Kwan Seum Bosal is a lovely, simple mantra that can be used to bring us into present time with the direction of compassion. In Korean temples, this mantra is the common practice of millions of women who chant to bring the mind to one point and awaken compassion in their life, and the lives of their family. This chanting is accompanied by a *moktak*, a traditional percussion instrument made of wood. Since we do not always have this specialized equipment on hand, we can use the fingers of our hand to beat time. Using the thumb, touch the tip of the pinky; recite the syllable "Kwan" (perceive). Touching the tip of the ring finger, recite the syllable "Seum" (world sound). Touching the tip of the middle finger, recite the syllable "Bo" (Bodhi). Touching the tip of the index finger, recite the syllable "Sal" (sattva). Try chanting this for ten minutes within a time you have designated for meditation practice, bringing body and mind, inside and outside, to one point by simply chanting. Just doing it. Then, as you chant, evoke the archetype of Kwan Seum Bosal—the compassion within us as well as the compassion all around us—recognizing these are not separate from each other. If there is a person or situation that would benefit from the healing energy of compassion, you can dedicate this energy to help their life. Now that you have this chant anchored into body-centered awareness, you can access this mindfulness practice when sitting in traffic, walking to a meeting, or any time when you wish to connect with the source of compassion.

Chapter 8

APPLIED ZEN:
CREATING THE
WORLD AROUND US

I spoke at the American Museum of Natural History in New York City a few summers ago, at a conference for elementary school teachers on creation myths. Every religion has a creation myth except Buddhism. So this situation initially presented a kind of cosmic humor. Yet, when we look into this, the Buddhist teaching on creation runs quite deep. What we teach is that we are always creating the world around us through our intentions and actions; at every moment, we have a choice. What world will we create? Every thought affects the world around us. In traditional Buddhist art, this teaching is represented through the Wheel of Life. The Wheel of Life shows various phases of the cycle of becoming: sensation, impulse, thought, action, and so forth. We can see these elements as contributing together to create the weather patterns of our lives, just as moisture, temperature, barometric pressure, and other factors contribute to snowfall. When we attach to a certain place on the wheel, such as a pleasant situation that we want to keep permanently, or an unpleasant situation that we cannot accept, perhaps triggering our reactivity, we suffer. When we are able to stay centered within these weather patterns, the coming and going of phenomena is simply the rhythm of life and the natural expression of our Bodhisattva path. There is a beautiful passage written upon a stained-glass window in the Oakland airport:

> There is nothing that involves only going without returning. It is the nature of Heaven and Earth. When there is going, there also must be returning.

This passage from the I Ching captures something that we innately know: arrivals and departures are one movement, separated only by the optical illusion of time. This installation is graced with eighty red-crowned cranes, signifying good luck and auspicious travel. The cranes add a lightness and movement that raises our spirits. Since the beginning of time, it has been like this: we are part of this movement, this grace. Like the cranes, we are practicing the arts of departure and arrival.

Zen Master Dōgen wrote about the way we create our world through the form of water:

> Dragons see water as a palace or a pavilion. Some beings see water as the seven treasures or a wish-granting jewel. Some beings see water as a forest or a wall.[1]

Where we put our eyes, what we choose to see, or not—through this, we create the world around us. At every moment, there are thousands of details of sensory input we filter out in favor of what is more stimulating, in a pleasant or unpleasant way. Very often, experiences that trigger fear receive high priority. The Buddhist word for mental patterns describes these as a rivulet, which follows the path worn by previous waters, the path of least resistance. Traditional Buddhist and Vedanta philosophy describes this process well. When a powerful emotion arises, then the *samskara* (the memory trace) that results will be heavily charged, and its seeds will be buried deep in the unconscious. When these charged traces come up, whether in response to a current situation or recognizably as memories, it is easy to bite the hook and become entangled. We get caught in an internal narrative and may speak or take action based on this storyline. This provides the samskara, with more fuel. On the other hand, if we are able to see that familiar pattern arise and not touch that hook, it loses force—and eventually loses its power over us.

To quote my teacher Debra Grace, "We can choose not to have the conversation of fear," a choice necessary for our well-being, which is supported by mindfulness. By choosing to focus on compassion and peace, we can create a world of compassion and peace. By seeing the wholeness within people and situations, we call that forward. Several studies have shown that when a teacher has high expectations of her students, she discovers those met; when a teacher has low expectations, students' performance drops in equal measure. My teacher Zen Master Seung Sahn had a tremendous capacity to see the potential within his students. When returning their letters, he often concluded by lifting this potential to their shared awareness: "I hope that you will soon finish your homework, attain enlightenment, become a keen-eyed lion, and save all people!" This encouraged students to go the extra mile and step into their innate wisdom. In this way, we can practice seeing our world with eyes of wholeness. This creates a sacred world within our here-and-now experience. This is tangible; it begins with ordinary people, you and me, and our basic sanity. When we are in traffic, breathing deeply. Making eye contact with a store clerk. Practicing loving-kindness in a challenging interpersonal moment, or simply disengaging—through which we return to our original luminous awareness like clear water. It all begins with us and how well we are doing in transforming our own passion into compassion and our own anger into discriminating wisdom. As my teacher Maha Ghosananda has taught:

A peaceful heart makes a peaceful person.
A peaceful person makes a peaceful family.
A peaceful family makes a peaceful community.
A peaceful community makes a peaceful state.
A peaceful state makes a peaceful country.
A peaceful country makes a peaceful world.

As we begin practices of mindful awareness and active co-creation of our life, we may sometimes feel overwhelmed. We may wonder how we can begin to create our destiny, or our shared future, when the ground we are working with is deeply challenged. There is a text within Tibetan Dzogchen tradition: "The mind which perceives the luminosity is the luminosity." Just so, the mind that perceives the beauty in nature recognizes this beauty because it is not separate from nature. This teaching is found within many indigenous wisdom traditions as well. The Thirteen Indigenous Grandmothers' Council, a group of elders who represent these ancient cultures, consider this part of the "original instructions" we are all born with. In the beginning of our culture—at the beginning of our own lives—perhaps we experienced a sense of this partnership, a sense of being part of the natural world, and that life force that creates everything. The challenge is to step out of our own way so that this luminous awareness can come through us. This pure potential exists within each of us, a luminous seed of Bodhicitta. It is the seed's responsibility to grow into the sprout and golden fruit it is intended to become. We are our own master; we are also our own enemy. The enlightened beings can help us, that's all. It's still up to us. We are responsible for creating our world. Our ability to awaken Bodhicitta depends on our own ability to accept and forgive ourselves. Therefore, the practices of compassionate abiding, as well as metta (reviewed in chapter 5), nurture the seeds of our becoming.

In the practice of compassionate abiding, we practice meditation with an intention to allow ourselves to actively contact and work with discomfort. Many people experience restlessness, itchiness, or other discomfort during meditation. Whether the discomfort is physical or emotional, our situation is essentially the same. Contact the feeling. Allow yourself to open to it fully, breathing it in. Breathe in and out, continuing to open and soften around it. As we sit, the body/mind releases energy. We may experience this release as a blessing, as bliss. We may experience the release as anxiety, restlessness, or itchiness. These are different aspects of the same phenomenon. Our renewed connection with our own life force, and the somato-emotional awareness of the body, is supported through unconditional acceptance of our body/mind unconditionally. This complete openness is the practice of the Lion's Roar. As we sit with this experience unconditionally, at that moment of not-knowing and of pure experience, our most difficult karma, our stuck place, is transformed into its jewel-like essence, its Dharma. Vipassana teacher Michelle McDonald describes this practice vividly:

> A few years ago, I did a retreat on the Big Island, and during the retreat the volcano erupted and I'd never seen it before; it was like this liquid fire just pouring up into the air. It was the first time in my life that I actually had the sense of this energy and how to work with it; it's just like the energy the earth has, and if you step out of the way, you can just let this energy come and go. It's built-up pressure, usually, it's heat and it's fire, and it's pressure and it's wonderful if you can get out of the way. It's usually not that pleasant, but it can be joyous just to feel it as an energy and let it come and go.[2]

While the catalyst is something outside us, the first essential work to be done is again, essentially, our own—befriending our own feeling, the primary cause that meets causes and conditions, and is triggered. As we do this, the external world already begins to shift in response.

I saw a wonderful archetypal description of this within Golden Gate Park in San Francisco one weekend. Arriving in the park, I found one tree just the right height and width for climbing. I sat on a branch, enjoying the wonderful companionship and groundedness of this tree. As I sat there, a cluster of children around the age of seven were playing tag and improvisational games in the forest grove, aware of my presence yet unconcerned. My seat within the tree provided the perfect vantage point from which to watch in stillness the scene unfold. They began using the tree as a home base for a game of tag and pleading with their dad to be an "ogre" again. When dad got fussy, the little girls were not fazed a bit, and everyone found a way to connect. Dad was tired, so he opted, instead of being an ogre, to be the guardian of the tree. Soon after this, they all went walking through the forest grove. There is a part of ourselves we come to know through these simple dramas, the exchanges we have with each other that reveal the play of duality. Within the forest grove that is our life, all these trees that appear separate are connected at the root.

> How could we forget those ancient myths that stand at the beginning of all races—the myths about dragons that at the last minute are transformed into princesses. Perhaps all the dragons in our lives are only princesses waiting for us to act, just once, with beauty and courage. Perhaps everything that frightens us is, in its deepest essence, something helpless that wants our love.[3]
>
> —Rainer Maria Rilke

Perhaps all the ogres we run into are, on a soul level, created through our request. As we embark on the evolutionary journey that is our life, someone will play the role of the ogre so that we may experience the great joy of seeing through the illusion of separateness and arriving home. Even these difficult situations that we experience may be seen as a way that we create our world. Knowing this, we may proceed with detachment, equanimity, and kindness, seeing every encounter as a gift for our spiritual growth.

Exercise: Ways of Seeing

At the end of the day, reflect upon each interaction you experienced. Looking deeply into these, reflect on the ways that causes and conditions come together to create our moment-to-moment experience. See each person you met as a teacher, recognizing that each person has presented gifts as well as lessons you might not have experienced any other way. Notice where you're still holding onto something; set the intention to let it go, calling your emotional and mental energy back into present time through awareness of the breath.

If there was a misunderstanding, you might envision a little bouquet of flowers at the person's door as a skillful means to release the day's events. It doesn't mean condoning whatever might have happened, just releasing it so that you can live fully and freely in this present moment.

Sit with this awareness of breath, consistently bringing the mind back until thoughts and emotions can be felt as eddies of movement within the wave of breath that sweeps through body/mind. These ripples on the surface of awareness are *also* simply the nature of mind.

Chapter 9
TASTE AND SEE

Invited to give a talk at a Unitarian Church for Easter, I began reflecting on the connections between Buddhist teachings on liberation and Easter with the poem "O Taste and See":

O taste and see

the subway Bible poster said,
meaning The Lord, meaning
if anything all that lives
to the imagination's tongue,

grief, mercy, language,
tangerine, weather, to
breathe them, bite,
savor, chew, swallow, transform

into our flesh our
deaths, crossing the street, plum, quince,

Chapter 9

living in the orchard and being

hungry, and plucking
the fruit.[1]

—Denise Levertov

There is a mystery that Easter celebrates, which is also within our Zen practice. Spiritual awakening comes through accepting everything, all the fruits of the orchard, bitter and sweet. Being able to enter our own dark night, our innate raw material—grief, death, hell—gives rise to the fullness of joy, the fullness of our interior spring. This raw material is compost for the rose of awakening. Through the practice of mindful acceptance, we touch a deep wholeness. Within this, we discover a new freedom: the release of our heart and mind from the self-limiting patterns that often restrict our capacity to love and to connect fully with our life. Through meditation practice, we open to things as they are. Tasting the bitter, we can fully savor the sweet.

This is especially relevant in these times of great change, as we are all witnessing huge economic and social transformation in the world. Through mindfulness, we can transform our emotions into profound and powerful action. Our grief can transform into deep compassion; our anger can transform into clarifying wisdom, the sword that cuts through delusion. We need to touch the darkness within; that is where our light comes from. In the midst of our tender, open heart that can hold our own pain together with the suffering of the world, we find the mystery of compassionate awareness, which is great love.

Part Three

SUMMER

The Blossoming
of True Nature

Through the practice of traveling lightly, we learn to step out of our own way, so that the radiance of original nature can come through us. This experience is the fruition of the path—it is the innate joy we sense when we see there is so much blossoming in our garden. The fruit is ripe. This moment is our perfect teacher, and we meet it with the fullness of who we are. It is summer.

At the moment that we completely give ourselves to the experience of practice, we are the breath. Our inside and outside become one, mind and body become one, we and the universe completely become one. The energy received through this experience of oneness, through connecting with nature, through everything that awakens our heart— is like sap running through the tree: it is transformed. As we allow ourselves to receive this light, we blossom and become the golden fruit upon the tree of life that we are intended to become. In this way the honoring of our authenticity and soul gifts is an essential part of our partnership with spirit in creating the world around us. Through the blossoming and ripening of our own gifts, all beings are nourished.

Chapter 10
CREATIVITY

These practices shift us back into a way of living that is in alignment with our heartsong, the song that is essentially ours to express. As Martha Graham put it:

> There is a vitality, a life force, a quickening that is translated through you into action, and there is only one of you in all time, this expression is unique, and if you block it, it will never exist through any other medium, and be lost. The world will not have it. It is not your business to determine how good it is, not how it compares with other expression. It is your business to keep it yours clearly and directly, to keep the channel open.[1]

Our practice is designed to help us move into this vitality, our true expression. We may then experience a new restlessness, a divine discontent, the itchiness of a snake breaking free from its old skin. As transpersonal psychologist James Hillman writes, the creative spirit "needs its share of beauty. It wants to be seen, witnessed, accorded recognition."[2] In Zen temples, creative expression has always been closely connected to Zen practice. Haiku poetry, calligraphy, landscape painting, raku pottery, and tea ceremony are some of the best-known gifts Zen has brought to world culture. In my own life, poetry and photography best capture the sparkling energy of the moment. There is an immediacy and conciseness about these that aligns with the practice of Zen. Here are a few poem-images that describe moment-mind.

Each cell of the wild iris
shimmers
traces back to source
through incandescent veins
transmuting light into light:
tiny sun—
swaying in a sea of green

trickling of run-off water
amid the brown leaves—
an uncomposed rhapsody
varying pitch by puddle-depth.

ripple
in a sea of marigolds:
toad-tracks.

Poetry brings about a deep state of mind-body integration. In its use of words, poetry gives us a sensory experience. Its rhythms and resonances weave the language comprehension functions of the left brain with the holistic, intuitive awareness of the right brain.

There is another way in which both art and mindfulness free us to experience moment-mind. They shift the way our cerebral cortex processes information. The cerebral cortex is actually quite thin, just six cell layers arranged in vertical columns. Sensory experience—the experience of light, for example—arrives first at the bottom layer. It is carried from layer six to layer five, and all the way through to the top layer, where it is felt and seen in vividness: *Ah!*

Memory-based processing begins at the top layer, moves to layer two, and all the way through from the top layer down. For instance, the mind's categorizing of "that's a flower" reflects this process. While the mind's ability to create categories is useful, it is always memory-based, and thus by definition, bored. If this is our primary experience, the cortex has imprisoned us.[3]

Art and mindfulness liberate the cortex to process sensory experience so that we literally see the world in a new way. We reconnect with the vividness of our direct experience. Our senses come alive. Sensory experience is always spontaneous, always emerging: *just this.* Beginning each day as if everything is a miracle. Making the ordinary, extraordinary. This is something that we can taste and see for ourselves. When I do walking meditation outside, the intention and attention I bring to my senses deepens my awareness of the world around me. I hear each note of the birdsong; I see the colors of the flowers, trees, and sky come alive. I feel my feet on the ground in a new way. There is a deep intimacy with the world, which arises through the senses. It is exciting to see this direct experience of moment-mind lifted up through neuroscience as a point of connection between body-centered awareness and the arts.

To describe creativity in its own metaphoric language, we could say that beauty offers a true reflection of our own wholeness: it awakens us to the potentiality of creating our world. In the words of the poet John O'Donohue:

> When we awaken to the call of beauty, we become aware of new ways of being in the world. We were created to become creators. At its deepest heart, creativity is meant to serve and evoke beauty. When this desire and capacity come alive, new wells spring up in parched ground; difficulty becomes invitation, and rather than striving against the grain of our nature, we fall into rhythm with its deepest urgency and passion. The time is now ripe for beauty to surprise and liberate us. . . . The wonder of the beautiful

is its ability to surprise us. With swift, sheer grace, it is like a divine breath that blows the heart open. Beauty offers us refreshment, elevation, and re-membrance of our true origin and real destination. In this sense, the Beautiful is the true priestess of individuation, inviting us to engage the infinite de-sign that shapes our days and dreams.[4]

Beauty nourishes us by awakening the heart. It re-minds us to express that authenticity that is at the core of our being.

EXERCISE: WALKING MEDITATION

We will now share the simple and beautiful practice of walking meditation. Within this, we will walk with full intention and attention; we will see how that trans-forms our experience of walking. As we are walking, we give ourselves to this action one hundred percent. We can bring ourselves to this one pointed focus by walk-ing in step with our breath, by bringing awareness to the leg muscles as they flex and contract, or by bringing awareness to the feet as they lift, move, and place them-selves on the ground. Whichever point of awareness we choose, we give ourselves to it completely, the way a bonfire burns, leaving no trace. We can practice this in a garden or along a forest trail to allow our senses to fully receive the beauty of the natural world. Try this for at least a half hour. As the mind wanders, gently bring it back, just touching the earth, hearing, seeing—coming fully to our senses.

This simple act of attention is a way of appreciating our lives. Mindfulness refines our awareness, which is vital to artistic expression. In poetry and other intuitive work, the sensations we are picking up are quite subtle; it is like walking into a dark room and looking for one's shirt. The better we know the room, the easier to find it.

Chapter 11

AUTHENTICITY

As our creativity exerts itself, we need to live from our spirit. Discovering the spontaneity of moment-mind, we free ourselves from the grid of memory-based experience. We attain what the great teacher Suzuki Roshi called "beginner's mind":

> The beginner's mind is compassionate, it is bound-less. . . . This is also the real secret of the arts: always be a beginner. . . . In the beginner's mind there is in-finite possibility; in the expert's mind there are few.[1]

This is a practice of navigating by trusting our direct experience, rather than staying with acquired maps of the terrain, conventional wisdom, the tried-and-true patterns that have created zones of safety. In the words of my teacher Zen Master Seung Sahn:

> Someone said, "The sky is blue," so you believe the sky is blue, but these are all ideas, other people's

ideas, which are all different from each other. Korean people say, "The dog barks 'Mung! Mung! Mung!'" Japanese people say, "The dog barks 'Wong! Wong! Wong!'" Polish people say, "The dog barks 'How! How! How!'" American people say, "The dog barks 'Woof! Woof!'" All people have different sounds, and all people have different ideas. [2]

If you want to know the dog's true sound, we need to ask a dog; he will give a good answer. That means to trust our own eyes, ears, nose, tongue, body, and mind one hundred percent. Trust our not-knowing, which is that subtle yet discernible voice of our true self, our innate wisdom. This inner voice requires active listening and a commitment of time and energy to be heard. When we do listen to this inner voice, it may surprise us. We may find ourselves going against the grain of familiar expectations. In my own life, the decisions I made to ride an ambulance, to practice Zen, to accompany my teacher Venerable Maha Ghosananda on a walk across Cambodia to bring about peace, these all were impossible, unfathomable to my family and to many of my friends. Luckily, I didn't wait around for approval. My trust in this inner voice of my spirit has always been strong enough so that my direction is clear. This has been reinforced by my teachers. Zen Master Su Bong underscored this in his Dharma talks: "If you are clever, you can fool most people. If you are really clever, perhaps you can even fool me. But you cannot fool your True Self." Even though appearances may suggest everything is on an even keel, we do know when our life requires transformation in the service of our own authenticity. This is the evolutionary journey that so many of us are awakening to, in these times of great change, which, as Kobun Chino Roshi notes, is hard climbing:

> The more you sense the rareness and value of your own life, the more you realize that how you use it, how you manifest it, is all your responsibility. We face such a big task, so naturally such a person sits down for a while. It's not an intended action. It's a natural action.[3]

Just as the acorn grows inevitably and beautifully into an oak tree, there is a natural movement towards light: a calling. Some of my own most-challenging creative blocks have occurred when I approach this calling, this sacred ground. On a vision quest, the cliffs are steep, and the climbing down, perilous. Defenses stripped away, practice becomes sincere. When, after fourteen years of residential training in Zen centers, I first envisioned working and teaching outside of this structure, it took a leap of faith. I was leaving the safe and familiar world that had nourished me for the unknown. I would need to find an apartment, arrange my own utilities, and manage all the accouterments of house-holding. At moments, this was terrifying—but beneath that anxiety, I could also feel myself coming alive in a new way and discovering capacities I hadn't realized I had. During this time, I made contact with this anxiety and the courage that resided in my body-centered awareness through a trapeze class, having won the spot through a lottery.

Trapeze class was an experience of absolute freedom and a chance to see the luminosity of mind like the rainbow after a storm. As I climbed the ladder, the amygdala and its primal anxiety kicked in. Upon arriving at the ladder, one is walking hand-in-hand with the realization that chaos is just a footstep away. This part of the class acted as a spiritual plumber's snake, clearing the subtle channels of any patterns of fear that may be stored in the body. At that point, I noted the mind and its acrobatics—and made a decision to rule this rather than be ruled by it. As I made that decision again on the platform, it brought the body awareness into a brief yet intense conversation with the mind. Grasping the bar, I was already leaning into empty space. As I leaped off the platform, residual fear burned off like haze by sunlight; through a quick photosynthesis it transformed into energy, precision, grace. Within this moment of flight, I felt a great joy, a sense of being viscerally alive and everything being far more present, like the sense of presence that comes in the midst of long retreats, though with greater emotional charge. Coming down, I felt relaxed and exultant. Hours later, I felt washed clean to the bone marrow, and everything was clear like the blue sky of morning. This kinesthetic memory was a powerful support over the next several months as I moved into new territory. Since then, I have continued to keep flexing new muscles, to leap and go forward in new ways—though perhaps not always this physically—trusting the infinite net of our interdependence.

As we venture out into new territory, we need to proceed with what Don Juan called "controlled folly," taking ourselves lightly. When the situation feels most serious, play is most essential. In traditional Tibetan monasteries, the head of the attendants to the master served as a jester to break down preconceptions and any self-importance as well. Bernie Glassman, a lineage holder in Japanese Zen, brings a clown nose to every Dharma talk; he'll put it on at some point, as feels congruent with the moment. As actively engaged as he is in leading meditation retreats in Auschwitz, in the Middle East, and on the streets, he knows that humor is essential to Zen practice:

> The key is pulling the rug out, saying things that cause people to drop their preconceptions. A red nose can do that, too. It's about not knowing, being totally open to what's going to happen. At that point, your mental constructs fall apart.[4]

There are also many playful stories about Suzuki Roshi. In one case, a student seeking advice came in. He confided that he could not stop snacking. Suzuki Roshi reached over, "Here, have some jelly beans." Playfulness is a natural result of metta (loving-kindness); it is an expression of connection as well as curiosity and a sense of safety. Play also amplifies these qualities, so that we experience greater joy, safety, and connection. It is another way of bypassing the ego to rediscover the rhythms of life as they move through us—to join the general dance.

EXERCISE: REMEMBER TO PLAY

When was the last time you played a board game, juggled balls, or sang full out? Maybe a trip to the beach is in order, or a visit to the aquarium. Sometimes I play with watercolor pencils and draw landscapes, writing short poems to accompany these. What reconnects you with your own spontaneous, playful spirit? If you have children, ask them for help on this one.

Chapter 12
ECOLOGY OF MIND

The rain falls everywhere
Coming down on all four sides
Its flow and saturation are measureless
reaching to every area of the earth
to the ravines and valleys of the mountains
    and streams
to the remote and secluded places where grow
plants, bushes, medicinal herbs
trees large and small
a hundred grains, rice seedlings
sugar cane, grape vines
The rain moistens them all,
none fails to receive its full share.

—Lotus Sutra

From the beginning of time, this path has included everything and everyone—within the infinite compassion of Indra's Net and the wholeness of Buddha-nature. Just as the rain falls in infinite different ways but has one taste, so in this way Buddha-nature is expressed in infinite different ways, and yet, to quote Dōgen:

> No creature ever falls short of its own completion. Whether large or small, its shadow never fails to cover the ground.[1]

So it is said that as the Buddha got up from under the tree, he exclaimed, "Wonderful, wonderful! Each thing has it; each thing is already complete." This is radically inclusive. Everything is intimately part of our ecosystem. On a spiritual level, this means having compassion for those parts of ourselves that are difficult to look at, seeing these as workable. Rather than pushing down these elements so that they are buried—and gain energy, as the shadow we project outside of ourselves—we can work with this rich material. As we do so, this mulch becomes our Dharma, our treasure. This "shadow work" is the razor's edge of practice, the pick-and-shovel work. As we sit meditation, we will experience anger, despair, shame, jealousy—the entire range of human experience. In these transformative times, there is no way to escape making contact with these feelings. A great shift happens when we deliberately make contact with these feelings, owning and acknowledging them. As we bring awareness to our anger and other primal emotions, that awareness magnifies its heat; the practice may feel unbearable, and the pressure to identify with the storyline of anger, to move from our witnessing mind into the drama, may feel unbearable. At the same time, we train in staying with it, letting it move through us like a volcano. That practice of keeping our seat in a hurricane is the practice of alchemy. We continue to train in staying open, asking ourselves, "What is going on for me right now, and can I be with it, completely?" That quality of unconditional openness turns garbage into flowers.

This ecology of mind is mirrored in our experience of the earth, our true teacher. We are coming to see that you can't really throw anything away. When our inner life is accepted as a whole ecosystem with everything that arises seen as workable, it becomes possible to see this wholeness in the faces of the people around us, in our communities and in this sacred earth.[2]

EXERCISE: TURNING COMPOST INTO FLOWERS

Begin with fifteen minutes of Centering meditation. Consider a challenge you have experienced, perhaps an early relationship, a shift in career path or other adversity. Look at this from the highest perspective, as a hawk circles high above the trees, seeing the entire forest. In what ways has that situation helped you discover your inner resources— gifts of tenacity, of knowing your own heart, gifts of compassion and empathy, gifts of insight and wisdom?

Chapter 13

ENCOUNTERING THE SACRED FEMININE

Within Western society, our disconnection with the earth can be historically linked to our disconnection from the sacred feminine. The ancient religions recognized that women's fertility made it possible for the earth to replenish and the tribe to continue. On the cliff walls of Arizona, a thousand-year-old petroglyph shows a woman's figure with her hair put up in spiraled braids signifying her coming-of-age. This gift of life was held up and celebrated. In Vedic tradition, the common name for the goddess, Bhavani, is rooted in the Sanskrit root *bhu*, meaning "being, becoming, living," which is to say that the goddess is identified both with the creative force and with the act of creation itself.[1] As a noun, *bhu* refers to space, the world, the earth. We enter this physical plane through our mothers. We all depend on that early experience of connection both for physical survival and for our emotional well-being, that primary experience of healthy attachment that is the foundation for healthy body/mind integration and the capacity for sustainable relationships.

Therefore, as we come to acknowledge the divine feminine, we are also creating space to honor the earth, our bodies as they are, our limits, our sensuality, and our sexuality. We honor these energies through our altar, which has a statue of Kwan Seum Bosal. I also offer a course for our Sangha on the divine feminine within Buddhism. I find that for women, especially, the power and energy of connecting with the divine feminine has the capacity to sharpen our perceptions of the awakened nature within our own body/mind and deepen our confidence in our potential for awakening. Through this sacred image, we begin to shift the social coordinates that describe our shared values. There are creative tensions in discussing Buddhism in relationship to the divine feminine. From a Buddhist perspective, all constructs, including gender, are seen as empty. At the same time, Zen practice and teaching shows us the nonduality of the absolute and relative: all phenomena, just like this, are truth. As Rita Gross, Grace Schireson and other prominent Buddhist teachers point out:

> The men who say let's not talk about gender because gender isn't real . . . don't go to the ladies' room, they go to the men's room.[2]

In meditation practice, as we make contact with "just like this" truth, and as we notice that all the faces in the altar paintings are men, we may feel hungry to see realization in a woman's body. This is not merely a search for resemblance, but a need to have our inner experience of the divine feminine mirrored. This is especially true on college campuses. When working with young women in a society that objectifies the feminine body, the presence of divine feminine images within Buddhism helps these women to see and know their own beauty. In discussing the archetype of the divine feminine with senior teachers across Buddhist lineages, we have seen that it takes innumerable forms. Some Tibetan teachings describe archetypal feminine energy as sharp, sensitive, quick to respond. These also describe archetypal feminine energy as empty.[3] In Buddhism, emptiness refers to the way that we are not separate from anything else in the universe. The archetype of the divine feminine in Buddhism thus can serve as a gateway to *prajna*, the wisdom of a way of knowing that is not separate from the known. To bring this connection between prajna, primordial wisdom, and the sacred feminine fully and concretely to the literal level, our core teaching on emptiness, the Prajna Paramita Sutra, is historically said to have been given first to Maya, the Buddha's mother.[4]

Looking deeply, we can see that this aspect of the sacred feminine exists within Buddhism as our gift from the indigenous practices that literally gave birth to the Buddha. Many goddesses figure in the sutras and traditional stories as nature spirits, celestial beings, and the earth herself. These images of the sacred feminine were part of Shakyamuni Buddha's world. Through the transmission of sacred texts that contain their stories, these goddesses are now part of our spiritual family.

It's also true that in many early texts, there is an ambivalent relationship to the body: women's bodies are referred to as sources of temptation and impurity. This reflects the primary experience of the writers as celibate monks, striving to avoid being distracted from their vows by feminine beauty. In this striving for purity, some valuable gifts of the sacred feminine that were sourced through Buddhism's ancient roots became deaccessed in certain times and places. Fortunately, there were women practitioners who renewed our connection to embodied knowing. In Tibetan Buddhism, this happened through women yogis who held their own dakini lineages, who were known as powerful teachers without whom a monk could not attain enlightenment. In Zen, there were wise women who attained the wisdom of lineage through their own life experience.

My favorite story about a woman's enlightenment is the story of Sul, who lived in China during the eighth-century C.E. She was born to a Buddhist family who frequented the temple of the great Zen Master Ma-Jo. One day when she went with her family to the temple, Zen Master Ma-Jo taught her the simple mantra Kwan Seum Bosal. Everywhere she went, she practiced her mantra: Kwan Seum Bosal when she was playing outside, Kwan Seum Bosal walking to school, Kwan Seum Bosal when cleaning the dishes. As she continued with this practice, she found herself chanting as she fell asleep. One day, Sul was washing clothes at the river. As the temple bell sounded across the river, the bell sound, the clothes-washing, and the mantra Kwan Seum Bosal completely became one. She had woken up; her realization was recognized by Zen Master Ma-Jo, and so she is part of our lineage. There is another story about Sul that takes place much later in her life. She is a grandmother, attending the funeral of her granddaughter, and she cries. The villagers who have gathered whisper among each other: "Sul is enlightened. She has already seen through birth and death, why is she crying?" As soon as she hears them, she stops, and responds:

> These tears are better than a sutra, better than chanting. When my granddaughter hears these tears, she will enter Nirvana. Do you understand?

Our Zen tradition is based on finding a correct relationship to each moment-by-moment situation. The relationship between a grandmother and her granddaughter is very close, and so the natural expression of that intimacy within this situation is to grieve. Our Zen tradition sees that human warmth and feeling are also part of the great Bodhisattva Way. There are no stories told about Sul in the middle part of her life, but I can imagine her having tea with her neighbors, offering them her wholehearted presence as a pathway to healing.

Through connecting with the body, we connect with this capacity for healthy attachment, emotional intelligence, kinesthetic awareness: an undivided knowing. Through the body, we also come into a deeper kinship with the earth and our place in the web of life. Compassion appears spontaneously as an expression of this deep wisdom. As we begin to revalue the sacred feminine, we step into the fullness of this body-centered awareness and open the gate to a deeper understanding of nonduality.

EXERCISE: COMING HOME TO THE BODY

This meditation is called a body scan. When I teach meditation for stress reduction, this practice is always everyone's favorite, as it brings a sense of deep well-being.

Lie down on your back, placing your hands on your lower abdomen. Feel the rhythm of the breath rising and falling in the lower abdomen. Notice any warmth or coolness within it, any pressure or tingling. Ride the waves of the breath; let it deepen.

After a few minutes of watching the breath, send your awareness of the breath through the legs into the feet. Notice the temperature of the air upon your feet. Breathe through the soles of the feet, through the arches of the feet, through the balls of the feet. Breathe through the toes, one by one. Notice any area within the feet where you may be holding tension and breathe through it, letting the feet be relaxed and at rest. Breathe through the calves of the legs, the shins. Notice where they are making contact with the ground. Notice any physical sensation that is arising. Shift awareness through the knees, breathing through the intricacy of the joint: the muscles around the knee, the tendons, the ligaments, the bones. Breathe through the thighs, noticing any sensation or any lack of sensation. Breathe deeply through them so that the entire leg is relaxed, heavy, completely at rest. Breathe deeply through the pelvic area; this is an area where we tend to hold a great deal of tension, especially if we have been sitting at a desk or in a car. So, breathe deeply through it: through the muscles, the bones, noticing any warmth or coolness, any pressure or tingling. Notice if there are areas of pressure or constriction within the pelvic area. Breathe deeply through these, releasing any tension you may find.

Shift awareness to the tailbone and the spine: breathe through the spine, vertebrae by vertebrae. See the spine as a string of pearls, breathing through each one in its turn—from the coccyx, through the sacral, the lumbar, thoracic, cervical—until the entire spine is relaxed and completely at rest. If the mind wanders during this exercise, gently bring it back to the spine and to the breath.

As we complete this, we shift awareness to our left shoulder, breathing deeply through it. This is another area where we tend to hold tension, so breathe deeply through it. Note any pressure or tingling, any warmth or coolness. Breathe through the trigger point, a point just below the shoulder blade at its center, which often stores energy. Breathe through any heat or tension. Breathe through the upper arm, noting where it is making contact with the ground. Breathe through the intricacy of the elbow, through the forearm. Breathe through the left hand, through the top of the hand, through the fingers one by one. Breathe through the palm of the hand, sensing where it is making contact with the breath in the lower abdomen. Dissolve your awareness of the left hand back into your awareness of the body.

Shift awareness now to your right shoulder, breathing deeply through it. Notice any pressure or tingling within it, any heat or coolness—any sensation at all. Breathe deeply through the trigger point, just below the right shoulder blade, releasing any tension you may find so that the shoulder is completely at rest. Breathe through the upper arm, noticing the texture of air upon the arm. Breathe through the elbow, the right forearm, noting any warmth or coolness within the arm. Breathe deeply through the tendons. Breathe through the right hand, which does so much for so many of us. Breathe through the fingers one by one. Breathe through the palm of the hand so that the arms are relaxed, loose, completely at rest.

Dissolving our awareness of the right arm back into our awareness of the body, shift attention to the subtle muscles of the neck. Breathe deeply through these. Breathe through and release the jawbone. Breathe through the inside of the mouth, through the tongue, the lips. Breathe through and release the space just above the lips, the nostrils. Breathe through and release the bridge of the nose. Breathe through and release the eyes, the space between the eyes. Breathe through and release the cheekbones, giving ourselves a kind of facial using the breath. Breathe through and release the brow, the top of the head, letting it rest and be completely at peace.

Shift awareness now into the lungs, feeling them expand and contract in tidal rhythms. Breathe through the deep corners of the lungs, breathing through and releasing any constriction you may find. Notice the heart beating; breathe deeply through it, sending the heart loving-kindness for all that it does for us. Let that loving-kindness spread throughout the entire body. Notice the sense of deep wholeness that arises. Realize you can tap into that at any time by using the breath. Thank yourself for taking these moments to nourish the body and mind. Then, as you are ready, roll to one side and sit up.

Chapter 14

INYOUN—CAUSE AND EFFECT

What I've seen, experienced, and believe is that we all have moments of our life that stand out, ineluctably: when an authentic path becomes clear, startling us with its sudden revelation. A man came to visit our Zen center with one of those stories. This man had had a dream that he was a stonemason at Hsi Lai Temple, a Chinese Buddhist temple in California. Before he had this dream, he had never practiced, never visited a Zen center. After the dream, he felt he should go there. He visited Hsi Lai Temple, and after strenuous training, ordained as a monk. In response, I told him how I had had a dream of coming to Mountain Spirit Center. When the *inyoun* (karma/cause and effect) with Mountain Spirit Center was complete, I began to have another dream, which brought me to write this book.

A monk friend, who worked from sunrise through the desert sun until nightfall building a temple, told me this story, dating back to his earliest days in Korea. He was having tea with our teacher Zen Master Seung Sahn, as well as a famous mountain monk who had made a profound, deep connection with practice through physical work. As the monk spoke about his work practice, my friend listened and connected. As he listened, an ember leaped out of the fire and onto the center of his robe, burning clear through his *kesa*—the cloth monks wear that represents their great vow of service.

The word inyoun is difficult to accurately translate since the English language does not have an equivalent word. In the Tibetan language, the term is translated as *tashi tendrel*, auspicious coincidence. This is an abbreviation from a Tibetan translation of the Pali, which conveys Buddha's original teaching of the law of cause and effect, *pratitya-samutpada*. When this exists, that comes to be. When this arises, that arises. When this ceases to exist, that ceases.

When we take a good look at this world and see how interconnected we are, we begin to understand how every action we take affects everything else. People often assume that the cause and effect should be direct and linear like a game of checkers. Sometimes cause and effect is multidimensional, transcending logic—like quantum theory, just beyond the bounds of what we know.

We do not always see the causation at work. However, when we meet conditions clearly with an appropriate and compassionate response, it sets an entire chain of events in motion that benefits ourselves as well as others, creating beautiful relationships. Inyoun is that miracle of close kinship at the first meeting—a chemistry like lightning striking.

The first time I visited Omega Institute, a holistic learning center, there was a double rainbow over the parking lot. I fell in love with this place at first sight. Over the following week, I resolved to return as staff. At meditation class, I discovered a Dharma friend who was serving as the meditation teacher; he introduced me to the Omega programming department, and the rest is history. I've returned to Omega as a meditation teacher for eight summers; this renews my reservoir and jumpstarts my creativity. Omega community deeply appreciates my teaching and healing work, and the way that I create sacred space. This partnership is a clear example of inyoun. This law of cause and effect can be considered a spiritual law, akin to the physics law of conservation of energy, which posits that energy cannot be created or destroyed; it simply changes form. In Buddhism we understand that the energy of our consciousness is interrelated seamlessly to the situations of our lives. When we do the excavation work of bearing unconditional witness to our heart/

mind, we liberate huge amounts of energy from our shadow—and gain the ability to be fully in present time. Our center becomes strong like a martial artist. We gain full access to our inner power. When we have not done the pick-and-shovel work, it is like setting a course for the East while heading West. We have some intentions—to write a dissertation, to create new work or find a new mate—but the inner compass is unsteady. For this reason, it is essential for all of us to find time to meet the demons we carry, to have tea with them, to get to know them so that these potent energies can become integrated and can become our allies.

Within the New Age movement, there has been a great deal of focus on the Law of Attraction. While it is true that our intentions are very powerful, especially when freed from the static interference of the subconscious, the law of cause and effect is far more powerful and wide reaching than that. Cause and effect means that we are all in this together; our survival as a species depends on each other. Cause and effect means that we are all connected throughout time, all manifestations of Original Nature—great love, which arises together with great responsibility. When we truly connect to the power of Original Nature, it breaks our heart open.

The simple truth is that every relationship in our life has a sacred dimension. As my friend Iyeoka Ivie Okoawo, a spoken-word poet, writes:

let that be my DAILY TESTAMENT
That ANY person I MEET at any point
can play a role in MY LIFE that can CHANGE the
DYNAMICS
of EVERYTHING.[1]

When our actions come from this vision of connection—
when we are aware that cause and effect seamlessly weave
the tapestry of our lives—we are likely to treat every visitor with kindness and tolerance. Each thought, each action, like a stone thrown into the water, creates widening circles.

EXERCISE: NAMASTE

Namaste means "the spirit in me greets the spirit in you." Recognizing that we are Original Nature, we also acknowledge that all others are also Original Nature. The ancient gesture of placing our hands in prayer position and bowing represents this; it is an expression of unconditional love through awareness of our shared divinity. We bow to see this true nature since the physical action takes us out of our head where our ego reigns. When this gesture is fully embodied, it is a letting go of any filters, any constructs that separate us from seeing clearly. It brings us back into a physical relationship that expresses this simple truth: when our lens of perception is clear, we see Buddha everywhere.

Try this: Find someone to practice with. To begin, both of you will place your hands in prayer position while standing. One person will keep this position. The other person will lower himself, taking a kneeling position, bringing the head to the ground, placing the hands on the other's feet. You who are the giver, allow yourself to send loving-kindness through your hands, as well as to receive through them. You who are standing, allow yourself to give loving-kindness through your feet, as well as to receive the other's reverence. Exchange positions, so that there is a balance between giving and receiving. This exercise has come to me through the spiritual teaching of Andrew Harvey.

Chapter 15
LISTEN

As we move into the practice of compassion, we discover how deeply it rests on listening. As we open the doors of perception, we are able to see, hear, understand, and touch another person; this is, to paraphrase the founder and pioneer of family therapy, Virginia Satir, the greatest gift we can give another. This is also the greatest gift we can give ourselves; through the active practice of listening, we access our tacit knowing, the kinesthetic awareness of the body. This tacit knowing is described in Zen training as "before-thinking mind." Through the body, we reach into a deeper reservoir—wisdom beyond wisdom—that reveals itself through synchronicities, dreams, and inner guidance.

So it is that when the pharmacologist Otto Loewi accepted the Nobel Prize in medicine, it was with the words, "I thank my dreams." The discovery of the experiment that led to groundbreaking work on the transmission of nerve impulses had come to him through a dream. The creative leaders, artists, musicians, and scientists of our time are those who have opened the gate to this liminal awareness. The challenge is simply to free ourselves: to listen, open, and trust. Through this practice of listening and being open to receive guidance from our higher self, we will receive the healing insight and vision that makes it possible to navigate this rushing river with grace.

In my own life, embodied knowing and tacit awareness have been essential allies. Through meditation practice, I align with "before-thinking mind." As I tap into this deep river, dreams and intuitions guide my path of service, revealing doors of opportunity where another person would not have seen a door. Dreams have also brought insight that reveals the meaning and purpose within my life. During a solo retreat in the forest, when all my senses were awakened, this dream appeared completely clear, in full detail, as if half of it were spoken to me, half of it seen:

A young man of a village wishes to become a healer. He needs to find a healing teacher. From a wise person in the village, he receives a scrap of gold lamé fabric and the words, "The greatest teacher will have exactly this fabric." So he sets out. He crosses river and mountain, traveling from village to village. Everywhere he goes, he inquires into the healing arts. When he hears of a healer, he goes to find them, inquires with his scrap of gold lamé fabric, studies together with them a bit, and then moves on. As he makes his rounds, people of the village who know of his interest occasionally approach him with their maladies. When this takes place, he politely explains that he is not a healer; he is only a student who is very dedicated to this search for this great teacher. Once he has found and studied with the great teacher, he will come back to heal them.

One day, a woman approaches him. Her child is sick. He begins to explain that he is just a student. "No," she says. "My child needs you now. He has a dangerously high fever." So the young man goes to her house, to the child's bedside. He tries every remedy, every technique at his disposal. He pours every inner resource, all the energy of his body and mind into the situation; his sweat mingles with the fever-sweat of the child. At the end of the night, the fever breaks.

The first light of dawn illuminates the room: the child and young man lying together on the bed, exhausted, and the child's receiving blankets, which are wrapped together with a swath of gold lame fabric. The young man has an awakening of insight: the great teacher, in fact, is the experience of pouring body and mind—all inner resources—completely into this situation. His heart, broken open by the experience, is able to receive the healing gift he had sought; healing light is drawn in and is able

127

to radiate forth. Thus it is that to serve is also to receive teaching.

This dream illuminated my own path at a time when my life was beginning a period of great change. The insight it delivers is to give myself wholeheartedly to my practice of service and trust in this as my teacher. Through this practice of trusting not-knowing, the healing gifts of compassion, wisdom, and authenticity are revealed. This message continues to inform every moment of my life, even as I write this book.

Synchronicity is another way in which nondual wisdom pierces the illusion of separateness to reveal the truth of our connection to each other and this world. Carl Jung defined synchronicity as a meaningful, acausal connection between inner and outer events, which spontaneously arises to advance the psyche in the service of a greater wholeness. Implicit within this is Jung's perception that psyche and the material world are not separate.

> Since psyche and matter are contained in one and the same world, and moreover are in continuous contact with one another and ultimately rest on irrepresentable, transcendental factors, it is not only possible, but fairly probable, even, that psyche and matter are two different aspects of one and the same thing.[1]

Through quantum physics, we have also seen that energy and matter are a swinging door that is in continuous motion. As we bring a kind of openness and curiosity to our lives, this dialogue between psyche and matter becomes more transparent. Synchronicity may arrive in ways that delight and surprise us, reconnecting us with a hidden wholeness through our sense of wonder. One of my especially rewarding moments within work this year included a synchronicity. We were beginning this year's Art and Soul coffeehouse series to nourish students' spirituality through the healing energy of the arts and the power of our shared stories. Our first performance of the year was taking place earlier than usual in the semester, advance publicity had been light, and I had not found a student to anchor the open mic, which followed the feature performance. We needed someone to energize and inspire the room. I stood outside the multifaith center, reflecting for a moment, just as one of our most-talented students walked by. I warmly greeted her and let her know about the Art and Soul performance. She hadn't realized the coffeehouse was taking place but decided to show up and bring a song. That evening she stepped into her own with opening words that underscored the transformative power of the arts:

> Last year as a first-year, I did open mic for the first time. Before doing this, I hadn't found a place here at Wellesley. But at that moment, I found my place.

As she sang "I Do It for Love," our world suddenly became much brighter, the room spellbound. My own sense of this is that true song draws from this deep river within. Through creativity, we express and embody a vision that is not only ours.

The poet John O'Donohue writes:

> The experience of the beautiful . . . is the invocation of a potentially whole and holy order of things, wherever it may be.[2]

True song connects with the roots of all art, the song of the world, which arises from the heart and awakens all beings. That sparkling moment was made possible by my own don't-know mind, the openness to an inner voice that prompted me to linger outside the performance hall briefly—just long enough.

> Out of nowhere, the mind comes forth.[3]
> —Diamond Sutra, trans. John Tarrant

In our contemporary Korean Zen tradition, we arrive at this same point through the phrase "don't-know mind." Within Zen training, we begin by emphasizing precision, posture, the forms of practice. However, these are simply creating a container within which we can rest our mind in its natural, spacious awareness.

The wisdom, clarity, and compassion we are looking for are already there. We just have to step out of our own way so that this grace can come through. So it is—there are moments in which we labor towards perfection, and moments in which we realize the infinite compassion that surrounds and nourishes us.

There are countless stories in Zen about monks who worked hard to attain enlightenment and then let go. A disciple of Zen Master Pai Chang went out from the meditation room into the yard to sweep the path when a pebble hit a piece of bamboo; his mind opened.

Here is a story about letting go that comes from one of my Dharma sisters in New York. Trish's daughter was getting married. Like many brides, she managed every detail of her wedding from the invitations all the way through to the reception. The one thing Trish's daughter did not plan for was the ride home since they live just two blocks from the reception. They walked to the wedding hall, and all went beautifully. When the guests had departed and it was time to go home, the skies opened—a downpour reminiscent of *Monsoon Wedding*. This was the one moment of the wedding that had not been planned. Trish's daughter went out to the curb to hail a cab. No sooner had she put her hand out then a stretch limousine pulled up; the passenger sprang out, declaring, "No bride is going to hail a taxi on her wedding day." It was Dustin Hoffman. He stepped out in the rain and turned the limousine over to the bridal couple for an exuberant ride home. As the limousine also contained family, it was quite full. He then walked towards his apartment.

Our practice is like this. There are moments in which we strive for precision, and there are moments in which we step into grace.

EXERCISE: LISTEN

Lost

Stand still. The trees ahead and bushes beside you
Are not lost. Wherever you are is called Here,
And you must treat it as a powerful stranger,
Must ask permission to know it and be known.
The forest breathes. Listen. It answers,
I have made this place around you,
If you leave it, you may come back again, saying
Here.
No two trees are the same to Raven.
No two branches are the same to Wren.
If what a tree or a bush does is lost on you,
You are surely lost. Stand still. The forest knows
Where you are. You must let it find you.[4]

— David Wagoner

Find a wildlife sanctuary, a forest, or another place where you can connect with wild nature. Give yourself at least an hour to wander its paths with all your senses awake. What do you see? What do you hear? What fragrance is borne on the wind, what is the texture of the earth underneath your feet? What medicinal plants grow nearby? What sound does the crow make; what is it responding to? What ecosystems of life are going on all around you? Check in with the kinesthetic awareness of your body. How does your pulse quicken in certain places, how does the rhythm of your breath change in response to its surroundings? What is the sensation within your belly telling you? How does that compare to the sensation in your hands, or the sensation within the soles of your feet? Try to see each tree, each flower, each leaf with fresh eyes, as if you have never walked in the forest before. When you finish this exercise, try to keep that same level of awareness within your everyday life.

Chapter 16

DAKINI, SKY DANCER

⌒

This awareness of the interplay between psyche and matter is expressed in Buddhist symbolic language by the five elements. While in the West we recognize four elements—earth, air, fire, and water—in the East there is a fifth element, the element of space. As Zen students, we begin practice with the recitation of the Heart Sutra, the core of the Buddha's teaching. The Heart Sutra describes the way that matter and energy, which Buddhism describes as form and emptiness, are always changing places. Waves come out of the ocean, crest, and break upon the shore, returning to the ocean. The autumn leaves became mulch and are already arriving as spring flowers. The element of space is that raw energy of emptiness before it takes form.

The element of space has a quality of vastness and limitlessness like the blue sky, which holds everything. It is this emptiness that makes it possible for everything to come into being. When we connect with the element of space, we attain a sky-like mind; we are one with this fifth element, the primordial energy of creation.

Thus, the primary archetypal energy of awakening is represented in Tibetan art as the *dakini*, whose name in Tibetan means "sky dancer," moving freely through the element of space. Dakinis are archetypally female, as the womb physically represents that emptiness that gives rise to all phenomena.[1] As the koan asks, "The sky is already blue. Why is there lightning?" Thoughts arise spontaneously out of the emptiness that is the nature of mind. Dakinis are naturally at home in liminal spaces—bardo realms, subtle energies, dreams, creation itself—understanding they are pure potentiality, one with the life force that creates everything. We, also, are this.

EXERCISE: SKY GAZING

This exercise comes out of Tibetan Buddhist tradition. At the end of your Centering meditation, go outside. Sit or lie down and look up at the blue sky. Let yourself become one with the sky. Let the sky be within you. Sense your mind as open and clear, as free and limitless as the blue sky. Rest in that natural spaciousness and clarity.

Chapter 17

APPLIED ZEN— COMPASSION IN ACTION

As we discussed in chapter 8, we are responsible for creating our world. When we step out of our own way, we discover the power, joy, and deep connection that is within this present moment.

There is a Hopi poem that speaks to this:

There is a circle here . . .
There is a web
A network
Strands connecting
Those who share the vision
Who feel the hope
Who sense the mystery
We touch life
We hear the planet's pulse
We work quietly

Chapter 17

Together
And alone
Each task
Each piece
Each a part of wholeness
There is a circle here . . .[1]

Through this poem, so many threads of our conversation come together. As we've said, our life is a mandala—a complete, undivided circle. Our mindful awareness encompasses everything; it is that wholeness that is the true nature of our existence. Our life is a net of luminous threads, connecting everything through interdependence; our practice is to see the connections. Our world is continually being created by our way of perceiving it. Therefore, it is essential to continually clear our lenses. When we practice traveling lightly and recognizing everything that arises as self-created, this cleanses our vision. We then have great power to choose how to create our life within the time and circumstances we are given. In the words of the poet William Blake,

If the doors of perception were cleansed
Everything would appear as it is . . . infinite.

Seeing with eyes of compassion and wholeness, we create a world of compassion and wholeness. As Sogyal

Rinpoche, a contemporary Tibetan master, teaches, "In the very act of interpreting the universe, we are creating the universe."[2] This ability to source from clear awareness is nourished by experiences of beauty and finding spiritual community as well as other practices of deep connection with our sense of hope. As we discover the luminous seed of awakening that is Bodhicitta, our everyday life becomes a vehicle for awakening. Compassion and wisdom arise naturally, and our own actions benefit ourselves and others. This gift of awakened heart/mind and its seamless function in the world is the great mystery. Through clear awareness, we see that all life is living through us. The oxygen that we breathe has been replenished by the trees. In this way they are as close as our own body; actually, there is only one whole body, no separation. Everything that is alive is breathing together with us. Knowing this, we work to express this insight through compassionate action. Step by step, this creates our world. This poem is a circle: it ends where it begins, with us—and the moment clear in front of us.

EXERCISE: CREATING OUR WORLD

For one day, make a resolution to meet everyone in your life with kindness. Let the car waiting in the driveway into the flow of traffic. Make eye contact with the toll-booth clerk. Reach out to a fellow classmate. Give extra patience to those people who press your buttons. Surprise someone with a random act of generosity.

Recently, a Tai Chi teacher waiting in line at a Dunkin' Donuts drive-in bought a cup of coffee for the person in the car behind him when he heard the driver honk. This set off a chain reaction in which the driver of that car bought coffee for the person in back of him—and it continued through the entire line. Studies have shown that when one person practices kindness, people three removes away become kinder. At the end of the day, write a journal entry, noting what actions you took and what effects you noticed.

Chapter 18

INTERPERSONAL MINDFULNESS—ZEN AND RELATIONSHIPS

~~~~~

At the heart of all relationships is an awareness of our interdependence. We know this through heart-to-heart conversations with our friends, and we sense it in the meditation room when sitting silently together. We've spoken of these relationships in earlier chapters as sacred ground through which we discover great love.

We're now going to look more deeply at interpersonal mindfulness, which is so often the creative edge, bringing vitality and depth to Zen practice. It's essential to remember that relationships are perhaps the most challenging spiritual work. This is precisely because we do continuously reflect each other, and what the other reflects back may be a facet of the self, which we are still learning how to love and acknowledge. Even if we offer each other the potential of a truly beautiful reflection of strengths, this may shift and change as we grow. If one's idea of love is situated around finding a missing half, as each person grows and changes they will discover those strengths they'd attributed to the other within themselves. Love that is based on keeping that constellation of feelings, which defines romantic love permanently and unchangingly, is a delusion—one that is common to our culture. My teacher Zen Master Seung Sahn counseled wedding couples with the phrase, "Only go straight ten thousand years, married." The direction of this spiritual advice is to give this commitment everything we have, to work to resolve differences together wholeheartedly. Very often, this is accomplished through simple, every-day actions: folding someone's laundry, getting up to make the oatmeal.

In order for us to sustain these actions that create sacred space for love, we need to draw them from a deeper well. It is necessary to find our treasure inside. We access loving-kindness by meeting the moment as a friend, and by being present to ourselves unconditionally. Out of this wholeness, our love then overflows; we see the beauty in another person, having first met it in ourselves. A marriage can then act as the vehicle for the expression of this great love in the world and provide deep, spiritual practice.

All our relationships, even those that are ephemeral, are the expression of our Zen practice. We are always coming into being with each other and this world. The practices of interpersonal mindfulness generate the most questions from my students. Relationships require that we know ourselves more deeply so that we can be a clear mirror for each other.

Seeing all relationships as a spiritual practice, how can we bring our deepest intentions and most impeccable integrity to this practice? How can this integrity honor our relations while at the same time allow us to be true to ourselves? We are called to express in partnerships that spirit of reciprocity that is our relationship with the divine. Our sitting practice is a wonderful teacher in this regard. As we sit meditation, we will experience periods of restlessness as well as perfect equilibrium. As we get to know our habitual responses through bearing witness to these—seeing them rise and fall a thousand times— we begin to strengthen our core relationship, which is with ourself. Our greatest treasure is inside. Each of us accesses it there. We access this unconditional love by making friends with each facet of our self. Then we can be independent; we can enter into relationships from a place of strength, sharing from the rich treasure of love that is within.

In ancient geometry, the symbol of the *vesica piscis* was used to represent both sacred space and sacred relationship. The vesica piscis, a shape formed by the meeting of two identical circles—the circumference of one intersecting the center of the other—resembles a fish; this is the source of its Latin name. The vesica piscis is an element of sacred geometry. When building a cathedral, the construction began with a vesica piscis measured in the dirt to set the proportions of the cathedral floorplan.[1]

On an individual level, the vesica piscis symbolizes the meeting of two people. Imagine each person, perfectly centered in the sacred space of their life, comprising one circle. When we truly connect, we are meeting each other from this place of deep integrity. Through this deep connection, a greater wholeness appears. The vesica piscis represents this ground of interconnection.

This ground of interconnection, as we all know, is dynamic, ever-changing. While metta (loving-kindness) is a practice of love without conditions, it is necessary to have healthy boundaries in relationships. Relationships do have conditions: with love comes responsibility. We are called to develop a love so grounded in wisdom that it is tolerant, resilient, flexible. Of course, we stay open to the possibility that our paths may diverge, and people do not have to be enemies in order to release each other. The commitment we are making is to let our relationship with the other serve as a sacred place in which we can explore ourselves in the presence of another and offer the potential for true reflection to one another. In this way, the love between two people may serve as a vehicle for their own awakening and the awakening of all beings.

Whether we are married or single, a lay teacher or monk, we are always entering into the sacred path of relationship. Like Kwan Seum Bosal, we hear the cries of the world, and our life becomes our response. Knowing that every action we take has an effect, we find ways to bring our practice of interpersonal mindfulness into each moment of life.

Here, I will offer a few skillful means for working with the practice of relationship.

The first element is very simple: breathe. When we are breathing deeply, we are capable of making contact with ourselves and others deeply. Too often, we find ourselves having some energetic experience that—given the nature of the mind—gets wrapped around a storyline that is the mind's invention. This process is well described by the Wheel of Life we explored in chapter 8. When we breathe deeply, we connect with our inner resources in the here and now. The second element: listen. Listening is like breathing, almost too simple—so simple that we miss it in the din of sound and stimuli that is modern life. Can we listen so deeply that we hear the space between the words, what is not said as well as what is spoken? Can we listen without interpreting, simply perceiving what is said? This is the greatest gift we can give our loved one. Third, can we find our own place of presence—the still point in the middle of our circle, that mandala that is our life? In order to meet another authentically, we need to know where we stand. The authenticity that arises out of the ground of our being provides a foundation through which we can truly make contact with another. Fourth, can we meet the other where they reside and view the situation through their eyes? When another person senses our attunement in this way, they feel witnessed and are very likely to turn around to see from our perspective as well. These elements of right relationship are expressed physically through aikido, the martial art that served as my gate to Zen practice.

It is very essential to note that mindful relationships involve an active, engaged peace and not the near enemy of active peace, which could be described as compliance. Modern stress often comes from not knowing how to express our priorities. One of my greatest mentors taught me how to say "no" creatively and kindly, using the phrase "I would love to, but I cannot." We begin from a place of unconditional awareness and acceptance of our feelings, just as they are, without judgment—and also without identifying with these energies or spiraling into a storyline. When we make contact with our feelings in this way, we then have a choice in how to relate to these emotional weather patterns. We can see the whole ecosystem of relationship, as well as our place within it. This opens up new vistas; we can see creative solutions that are mutually beneficial from this place of equanimity. Body-centered awareness is key. In these challenging moments, take three deep breaths. Bring the breath through the body, as we've done with the body scan. When we shift our awareness in this way, we return to the center of our circle. As we shift our attention and awareness, we are actually shifting our perception and our worldview. When we note the feelings and thoughts that arise without editing these and without acting out, it frees up a tremendous amount of energy. This practice broadens awareness from the dominant discourse of primal emotion to a far more creative, integrative way of seeing. As we see this interpersonal moment with eyes of wholeness, we are then liberated to see its highest resolution.

EXERCISE: SEEING ECOSYSTEMS

Bring to mind a person with whom you have some difference of opinion. See them within their ecosystem, which is woven like a tapestry of threads of connection. These threads are variously textured: strong fibers of culture, race, religion; bright and dark threads representing family; gold and silver threads representing mentors, teachers, and friends; fibers that connect to the geographies of their lives; threads that represent every condition and experience—the fabric of life itself. Notice how the individual is comprised of all these threads woven together, many causes and conditions coming together.

Step back to see this tapestry in its entirety. Give this a few moments.

Reflect on the vast and subtle workings of cause-and-effect, which have brought you together in this place and time. This person, too, brings exactly what you need to awaken in the timeless here and now.

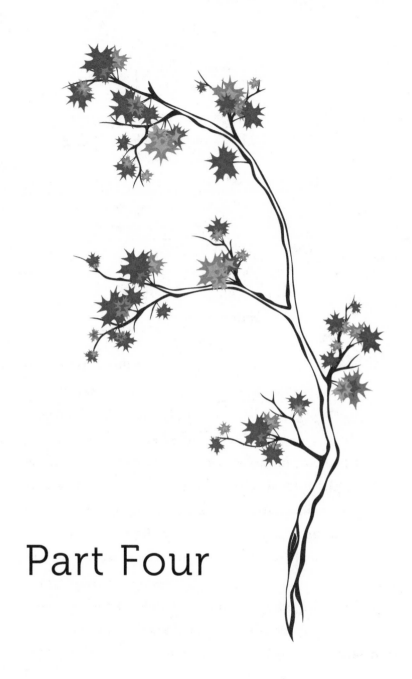

Part Four

AUTUMN

Everything Changes

Autumn, dusk.
everything changing.
And feeling how the sap itself
is returning to the roots,
back into the source.

Autumn is the best Zen teacher—its beauty is refined to
bare essentials, and its message is to the point: everything
changes. We gather the fruits of the harvest with joy and
gratitude, and return home with bliss-bestowing hands.

In September, East Asian communities celebrate the
mid-autumn festival with the arrival of the bright, clear
autumn moon. There is a Chinese saying, "When the
moon is full, mankind is one." Seeing the bright, clear
autumn moonrise above the trees, what we intuitively
sense is the wholeness of our being—and our kinship. We
and all other beings are together under the same moon.
Thus, the proverb. In truth, mankind is always one, even
in a new moon when the sky appears dark.

Chapter 19

WHOLENESS AND THE IMPLICATE ORDER

Through the wholeness within, we perceive and touch the wholeness around us. There is a tangible way that spiritual practices of connection actually create a fertile ground, which nourishes the development of insight. The direct correlation between the practice of compassion and awakening of self-insight is reinforced by cutting-edge work in the field of neuropsychology and the insights of modern physics. In the words of educator Parker Palmer:

> The true model of reality within physics is now seen to be relational. Atoms are not considered to be discrete entities, but a set of relationships reaching out to a set of other relationships.[1]

The way to know a connected universe is through being in connection ourselves. Through the quantum physics model of participant-observer, we know that observing an experiment already shifts its outcome. In another fascinating discovery, it has been found that when subatomic particles are split in two, the two parts will act as mirror images: one rotates clockwise, the other counterclockwise. If these particles are separated by a mile, and one is set to change the direction of its spin, the other also—instantaneously—changes.[2] Our connection with each other, through practice, can be clearly seen the same way. David Bohm, a modern physicist, wrote of these philosophical correlations. In *Wholeness and the Implicate Order*, he stated that all phenomena form an explicate order that we know as objective reality. These disparate phenomena all rest upon an implicate order, an underlying wholeness. In recent writing, Bohm went on to make the connections between the macrocosm and the inner world more explicit:

> The mind may have a structure similar to the universe, and in the underlying movement we call empty space there is actually a tremendous energy, a movement. The particular forms which appear in the mind may be analogous to the particles, and getting to the ground of mind might be felt as light.[3]

The explicate order of the mind referenced here would be an individual's conscious, discrete thoughts. In Zen practice, we refer to this as the world of form. The implicate order is that original energy—luminous awareness itself—the ground from which everything arises. In Zen practice, we refer to this as *emptiness*. This brings to mind the Third Zen Patriarch's classic poem, "Sandokai":

> The spiritual source shines clear in the light;
> the branching streams flow on in the dark . . . [4]

This verse is chanted each morning by Soto Zen students. *Sandokai* can be translated as "merging of difference and unity," though this translation is hard-pressed to capture the nuances of Sandokai: best to sit with it for ten years. These two lines describe the explicate and implicate order of reality; in other words, form and emptiness.

When describing form and emptiness in Zen—as in all Zen teaching—we convey the essence directly through images, paradox: darkness and light. Zen is like jazz—it works the spaces between the notes—and we develop an ear for that silence through sitting meditation. Within that deep listening, we touch the knowing that is within our entire body and mind. Practice develops our innate subterranean tacit knowledge, our connection to the ground of being. Working with a great question, through koan study and the study of teaching verses like Sandokai, helps us access these levels of knowing consciously. These practices of working with paradox are designed to derail our linear thought so that we can connect with a deeper process, which is the core of Zen.

These two lines of poetry describe an inner process. For every word that is written, there is a depth against which our oars strike: an inarticulate, tacit body of knowledge that is coming to light. The process of evaluating a work of art, or composing music; the breakthroughs which characterize great science, such as Kekule's discovery of the shape of the benzene molecule; the art of relationship, which characterizes transformative therapy—all these depend upon tacit knowing. Through meditation practice, we gain greater access to these subtle, subterranean ways of knowing. Parker Palmer notes:

> If we did not have bodies and selves that "indwell" the physical phenomena of the world in an altogether inarticulate way, we could not know any of what we know at an articulate conceptual, logical, empirical level. [5]

Knowing depends on not-knowing. Conceptual awareness depends upon mindfulness grounded in the body. The more precisely and thoroughly we come to our senses, the more we can attain a wide range and depth of vision and insight. If we would honor this emerging necessity in this postmodern age of creating a regenerative society, we need to trust and rediscover this unbroken wholeness within ourselves.

QUESTIONS FROM THE SANGHA

In Zen training, we teach using questions that push us past the edge of our knowing to the place before questions, our original mind. These great questions are found within all world cultures; they arise from the great mystery. Within Zen, we return the immense gift of these questions with another question.

Walking into a room to give teaching, that great question is my true reference point: that open space of not-knowing is the only place from which any authentic Zen teaching can arise. I have an outline and some simple meditation that is prepared. Then, I try to stay open and curious together with whoever is present—and simply connect.

When I was teaching in a bookstore in California, two kids came in. At that time, I was speaking about our human condition. "Trees understand their authentic path, their 'job,' and manifest it wholeheartedly. Birds fly, fish swim—all animals understand their job. But we human beings have a bit more work to do; we have a big job."

One of the boys asked, "Why do human beings have this big job?"

So I said to him, "Why are we here? Why are we alive?"

Chapter 19

"Why ARE we alive? I don't know!"

He really didn't know. He had already come in with a big question that was asking itself. So he asked, "Do you ever get the answer to your big question?" along with a few other wonderful, huge, wide-open questions like that. These questions are a huge gift in breaking open our preconceived notions of the world, the box that we get ourselves into through linear thought process. There is a Hindu proverb: "The mind of measure cannot know God." When we free ourselves from that finite process, we touch the infinite, that wisdom and compassion that has always been there. For this reason, in Zen training, asking questions is an expression of love. These questions are a way of seeing the luminous nature within each other and drawing it forward.

On another day, I gave consulting interviews at the Zen center. A young man I had worked with came in. He had spent a couple of years in the Peace Corps since I had last seen him. He asked, "How can I help all beings?" and "What is my true self?" I told him these are the same question. When we ask how we may be of service, in that very moment, our true self is revealed. Our true self cannot be put into words. However, this student's first question—its direction of love and compassion—is a powerful hint.

Recently, I gave a talk at Boston College. I spoke to the students about how we are never separate from the light of awareness—we are that wholeness.

156

A student asked, "If there is originally no separation, we are that wholeness—then why do we forget that? Why do we go through these experiences of pain and loss in everyday life without a full capacity to see through this? What is the point?"

I answered, "Perhaps consciousness comes to know itself through us—through this illusion of separateness that is *maya*, the play of duality—and through that process of discovery, there is a greater joy in arriving home."

PRACTICE: WORKING WITH A GREAT QUESTION

We all have a great question that directs and shapes our life path. It could be, "Where do the sun, moon, and stars come from?" Or "What is great love, and how can I find that?" Or "How can I make a difference in this world?" All these questions return to one question, which is "What am I?" Korean Zen is centered on this practice of meditating with a great question.

EXERCISE

Connect with the rhythms of breath using the Centering exercise. Begin Sitting Zen, bringing awareness to the rhythms of breath in the tandien. Count the breath, or use a repetitive phrase, for instance, *clear mind, clear mind,*

clear mind, don't know. As thoughts arise, ask yourself,
"Who is thinking?" Respond to yourself, "I am thinking."
Ask yourself, "What am I?" and respond, "Don't know."
Rest in that not-knowing. When an emotion or another
thought arises, repeat this process. Let your sense of that
ground of presence, that pure energy, deepen. This is our
original nature, awakened heart-mind.

This practice is one I learned from Zen Master Soeng
Hyang, the first woman to become a Zen Master in our
Korean Zen tradition. When you've tried this within formal practice, then try carrying this into everyday life—
meeting the moment with complete sincerity, asking
yourself, "What is this?" Through moment-to-moment
practice, we *live* our great question: living with passion
and presence, awakening in each moment to what is.

Chapter 20
WRITING WITH WATER

When I was teaching a course on Zen and creativity, we began together sitting in a meditation room with sumi ink brushes, drawing upon newsprint with water. Within moments, the lines disappeared. Nothing to attach to. The lines of our own lives are written in water. That impermanence is both our grief and our hope: true freedom that is freedom to grow into our own radiant compassion, our own completeness, our own path with heart. Which is then, like everything beautiful, not only ours.

> All paths lead nowhere, so it is important to follow
> a path that has heart. A man of knowledge chooses
> a path with heart and follows it; and then he looks
> and rejoices and laughs; and then he sees and
> knows.[1]
>
> — Carlos Castaneda

This is a powerful moment with the accelerated sense of time, amidst the great change that we are experiencing, to envision—in image, speech, practice—what is our path with heart? And to begin, as a gift to ourselves and to all beings, to embody it through meditation and clear action.

On a recent trip to Los Angeles, a friend drove me through Hollywood to Burbank Airport at dawn. Billboards jumped across our line of vision, itineraries flashed across the mind. A windstorm had knocked palm fronds across the roads, and now it was jostling the luggage in the truckbed: mind in ten thousand places.

Suddenly, we heard NPR on the radio interviewing Thubten Jinpa, the Dalai Lama's translator:

> There are certain key spiritual values that are at the core of Buddhist tradition—for example, the respect for all sentient beings. And the recognition that at the fundamental level, all beings have a natural disposition to aspire for happiness and overcome suffering. Similarly, the recognition that at a very deep level, everything is interconnected. That all events come into being as a result of causes and conditions.[2]

On a very deep level, everything is interconnected. All events come into being through causes and conditions. Hearing that, I realized that if you understand this, you understand all the teachings of the Buddha.

At that moment the billboards, the rehearsed sequence of departure and arrival, the illusionary landscape of Hollywood all receded into dream, mind returned to one point. At every takeoff and landing, I feel impermanence rest upon my shoulders, as close as an in-flight blanket. That morning, as the plane took off through a windstorm, just clearing the San Gabriel Mountains, I also felt held in luminous awareness. I imagine the bardo, the travel between lives, is just like this. In the midst of a thousand things, our own inner landscapes, may we all receive this grace, may we all awaken: everything is interconnected, all events come into being through causes and conditions. May we all receive this postcard from moment-world.

JI JANG BOSAL

The Bodhisattva who helps people through transition to the other side is Ji Jang Bosal (Jizo). Jizo is also the Bodhisattva of women, children, and travelers: all those who through their positionality are aware of the ephemeral nature of our lives. The heart instructions, when one has died, are to remain centered, calm, undistracted by the images that appear, seeing all these as our own radiance. Seeing every being as a being whose essence is compassion.

This compassionate awareness is the archetype of Jizo within us: the curiosity we opened to so easily as a child, the energy of falling in love, of going on a vacation, of looking up at the stars. As we practice and our consciousness becomes clear, this compassion begins to resonate so strongly and deeply that like a magnet it supports others, drawing them into alignment with their essence.

In the Korean Zen morning bell chant there is a beautiful poem:

> Holding these beads, I perceive this world
> with emptiness as the string,
> there is nothing unconnected.[3]

Compassion born out of nondual awareness connects all phenomena like mala beads upon a string, and it is the realization that we are already connected more deeply than we can know. This essential bodhicitta (awakened heart-mind) is what continues after death and illuminates our path.

In working with and really attaining an appreciation of impermanence, the most powerful teaching has been working with the dying. As my teacher Zen Master Seung Sahn said, "Two kinds of people. Soon die and later die." Working with the dying brings us face-to-face with our own death; it helps us get out of our own way in order to live this wild and precious life with grace. As I noted earlier, my first explorations of career and vocation offered this valuable training. My first job out of college was managing the office for an acupuncture clinic for AIDS patients in Boston's Back Bay; its executive director and many of its clientele died within the span of a couple of years.

In that same time span, I regularly visited Carlos, an eclectic campy Dharma student with AIDS who used art as a way of connecting with Buddha nature. He created large drawings of Amita Buddha, done with incredible precision using magic markers, so that his entire apartment became a Pure Realm. That taught me something about practice. It wasn't based upon my aesthetic but upon one pointed try mind—*just-do-it*—and compassion. Carlos trusted me as he had trusted few other people, and he made me the executor of his will. All of his temple accouterments—altar lamps, statues, sacred images—were carefully designated to specific beneficiaries and Dharma centers. The night he passed away, his estranged mother and her boyfriend arrived at the house with the spiritual bearing of magpies. With great dispatch, they carted off everything in the apartment for resale. That was also a great teaching: death is a complete letting go. Even the temple Buddhas and Bodhisattvas are gold dust. To quote a great teacher, although gold dust is precious, when it gets in the eyes it hinders the vision.

When Carlos passed away, I began volunteering at a hospice—helping with everyday tasks, covering the kitchen, sitting with the dying. The work was simple; the presence of death heightened my practice of mindfulness. I found that by bringing awareness into each moment, that openness awakened my heart. Pain was transformed into compassion. That moment of transition, as raw and unsettling as it is for all of us, is often at the same time quite beautiful, like the last glimmers of light upon the water, like the ocean's edge. And it may also bring peace— a welcoming home.

PRACTICE: HEART-CENTERED CLOSURE

This meditation is based on *phowa* practice, the Tibetan practice of preparing to attain the highest level of awareness while transitioning through death. It is adapted from Madeline Ko-In Bastis' *Peaceful Dwelling*. We can do this for ourselves as a way to experience a deep letting-go. We can also practice this with a loved one as a way of helping them to die consciously. We can do this on behalf of a loved one, envisioning them within this sacred space at the time of their passing, or within our meditation practice at some later time, as a way of coming to closure.

We begin by connecting with our breath, practicing mindful awareness so that we are centered in the body and clear in the mind. Envision yourself as whole and strong, radiant, joyful—in some place which is beautiful and reminds you of the sacred. Above us is the source of love, wisdom, radiance, Buddha nature . . . whatever name we may give to it.

Whoever needs to forgive us has done so. We are extending forgiveness to whomever there is to forgive. If we like, we can use these phrases:

> For all the harm I have done to others, knowingly or unknowingly, forgive me.
> For all the harm others have done to me, knowingly or unknowingly, I forgive you as much as I can.
> For all the harm I have done myself, knowingly or unknowingly, I forgive myself.

Through this practice we experience a cleansing of the heart-mind. In this way the source of love—the one pure and clear thing—is so touched that the light from above radiates into and through us, entering our heart, suffusing through our body, our arms and legs, our toes and fingers . . . and finally our head.

We are completely filled with light. We have become that light, one with the source of joy, one with great love and compassion.[4]

Chapter 21

PRACTICES OF RECIPROCITY AND GRATITUDE

This moment of life is too essential for anything other than gratitude.

—Stephanie Flanders

At the end of our Zen retreats, we always close with a circle talk, which is an opportunity for each person within the circle of retreatants to share something of their experience of the retreat. There are images that leap into mind—touching, wry moments—but overwhelmingly the energy that is expressed is gratitude. Gratitude to the retreat leaders for encouraging us and sharing insight. Gratitude to the head Dharma teacher and other retreat staff for creating this sacred space. Gratitude to our fellow participants for having served as companions on the journey. Perhaps, all of these summed up in a deep bow with hands palm-to-palm in the gesture we refer to as *hopchang*. That expression of gratitude is not an intentional action; it's a natural action. When we remove the filters that prevent us from being fully present, we see how everything is connected to everything else, that this entire universe is supporting us. What arises out of that insight is gratitude. Spiritual practices of gratitude are at the core of many indigenous practices; within traditional cultures, it is recognized that everything we bring in comes about through relationship. As Australian Aboriginal elder Bob Randall has pointed out, there is innately a connection of both love and responsibility between us and creation. When the balance is attended to, when we come into harmony, we all benefit. Through practices of reciprocity and gratitude, we return to wholeness with all that is, and reclaim our place in the family of things.

Ritual is a powerful way to celebrate and lift up the gifts we have been given. Zen Master Seung Sahn taught that the four elements give us everything we need for life, everything that makes up our physical body. So we are also nature: *we are the universe, and the universe is us.* We express our gratitude symbolically by placing the four elements on the altar. The incense burner, filled with sand, represents the element of earth; the incense itself represents air; candles represent fire; and there is an offering bowl of clear water, which is renewed daily. This is the starting-point for the ongoing practice of gratitude that is our life.[1]

Mindfulness strengthens our awareness of the blessings always pouring forth. Extending that appreciation through active practices of *How may I help you?* grounds our life in mindful awareness so that the earth itself is our altar. There are active practices of kindness we can take up, as well as tangible practices of connection and sustainability. Colin Beavan, the author of *No Impact Man*, is a teacher in our Zen school. He decided to commit to one year of living with as little impact on the environment as possible—no electricity, television, elevators, newspapers, cars—as an experiment in living in harmony with all beings and this world. This goal required some compromise since it affected his family, who are also part of these circles of connection, and with whom he also needed to make harmony. This deep practice was transformative. Colin now travels across the country to share his experience as a way of empowering people to see that their everyday actions are powerful means of change, and to build sustainable community. Not all of us can abstain from electricity for a year, but all of us can take steps towards a more sustainable lifestyle that makes well-being possible for future generations.

At Wellesley College, a group of students, faculty, and staff has organized under the acronym WEED. They have found ways to make huge campus events, which use large amounts of disposables, more sustainable through purchasing cutlery made of corn and providing compost stations. Also, campus printers have been reset to provide double-sided printing. And a group of students has established a sustainable farm plot where they learn and teach practices of regenerative agriculture. All of this builds a richer soil for our community with more possibilities for our shared growth. As Evelyn Rysdyk, a scholar of Andean spirituality, notes, "In traditional indigenous practices, people don't expect to receive what they are unwilling to give."[2] As we express our gratitude and compassionate action in the world, this great love, like a stone thrown into the water, ripples out across our widening circles of community—and also, these ripples return to us. Whenever we grow tired of saving all beings, we can listen to the birdsong, the crickets, the sound of a frog leaping into the pond, and recognize that all beings are already saving us.

From a Zen perspective, the important thing is to recognize that we are already complete. The birdsong, the crickets, and the sound of water return us to direct awareness of how intimately connected we are with the world around us, and that our true treasure is inside. When we recognize this, we naturally make decisions differently. We recognize that we don't need to buy the latest designer jeans or the newest smartphone to feel complete. Through paying attention to our actions, our speech, and our mind, we begin to see that the search for completion through material things is delusion—a cycle of craving that by its nature can never be completed.

There is a story told by my teacher Dae Bong Sunim about a dog. Sometime in the early days of our Zen school, a group of Zen students went to the greyhound track together. Within the race they were watching, there was a dog named Clear Mary. The Zen students appreciated this name; they bet on Clear Mary. Before the race, the greyhounds lined up expectantly. As the racing bell went off, the mechanical rabbit at the top of the fence began moving, and the dogs began chasing the rabbit—which was always just a little bit ahead of them—around the circular track. As the dogs lunged forward, the rabbit moved just a bit faster, always just out of reach. As the race continued, Clear Mary looked forward and then looked back. She looked forward again and looked back. Then she did something no other dog has done: she ran back against the current of racing dogs, tracing the circuit. She caught up with the mechanical rabbit and seized it in her jaws. The race was over.

In that same way, we are culturally conditioned to seek fulfillment through things, which is a subtle violence to the wholeness we already are. By spending our energy and resources on the latest plasma screen TV or the Kate Spade handbag, we are reinforcing a cultural trance of unworthiness. If we spend all our time seeking wholeness outside ourselves, when will we find our way home? True happiness is not found through these things but through inner peace, based on "enough mind" as well as love and compassion.

This emphasis on consumption seriously affects our relationship to the environment, and through the environment, the lives of all sentient beings who depend on the earth's ability to renew herself. Those three-dollar "doorbuster" toasters at Target do not cost $3 to manufacture, neither will they cost $3 to dispose of. The true cost is borne by the communities in which iron, rare earths, gypsum, coal are being extracted from the ground; the communities who breathe the factory air; the communities located near transfer stations, who witness hundreds of garbage trucks move across their street each day and breathe their diesel fumes; the ecosystems directly affected by landfills and our future generations, who will know better than we do that nothing thrown away actually goes away. When I asked his Holiness the Dalai Lama what the one thing is that we can do for world peace, he laughed. "It is not so simple. There is no one thing. But to do one thing—begin with ecology." [3] Each of us can recycle, save energy, simplify our lifestyles. Through this a future will be possible for the next generation. As we adopt practices of sustainability, our everyday life practice becomes wholehearted like a bonfire—leaving no trace. Through this, we enter into alignment and sacred relationship with all beings and this earth.

EXERCISE: PRACTICES OF RECIPROCITY AND GRATITUDE

As Pema Chödrön has said, mindfulness is already an expression of appreciation for the blessings always pouring forth. So, already within meditation practice, our sense of gratitude is present. And yet, ritual is so powerful a support in fully embodying this appreciation. In the creation of an altar, we are repaying the universe. We are also creating dedicated sacred space, which will serve as a physical reminder of our commitment to waking up and a sanctuary for our spirit. Find an image or statue that represents Buddha-nature, our awakened heart-mind. Place a candle in front of it. Find some incense that is scented in a way that evokes the sacred for you; place the incense burner in front of the Buddha. Find a container for the water offering: in Korea, these are traditionally brass, but a porcelain bowl also works beautifully. Change the water in this bowl each morning when you sit down to meditate; this is a way of bringing fresh energy to our sacred space each day. You may choose also to offer fresh flowers, rice, fruit, or other gifts of appreciation to the sacred. And there may be stones and other objects from nature that speak to us, which we may choose to include on our altar. Keep it simple, uncluttered; this space is symbolic of our original clear mind. By offering this beauty and praise to the sacred, we are expressing gratitude for the miracle of moment-to-moment life.

Chapter 22

MAKING THE CONNECTIONS—ZEN AND THE MIND

This capacity for centering oneself is both the foundation of meditation practice and the effect of mindfulness meditation; yoga, music, and other integrative practices also support the development of this capacity. Our emotional self-awareness and centering capacity is also the basis for empathy—being about to perceive the inner experience of another and responding with compassion. Through mindfulness practice, we've experienced this. Now, so that we can fully appreciate the gifts of embodiment and integration, we will explore the science of mindfulness.

The middle prefrontal cortex serves as a keystone of consciousness. Many of the functions we would consider essential to higher awareness are overseen by this area: the ability to communicate through symbolic forms of information; modulation of fear; emotional balance;

response flexibility; empathy; attuned communication; self-insight and narrative; moral awareness and intuition.

The prefrontal cortex is also unique in that it makes connections to the limbic system, the brainstem, and the rest of the neocortex. The brainstem and limbic system together represent those regions of the brain that carry out basic survival-level functions. The brainstem carries out hard-wired activities like heart rate and respiration. The limbic system is the region of the brain connected to primal emotions, body-centered awareness, and early life experience. By bridging the functions of our instinctual self with our conscious self, the prefrontal cortex brings these parts of ourselves into conversation with each other, and therefore plays a key role in the process of vertical integration. The high level of bidirectional flow of information between the limbic and prefrontal areas creates a feedback system to promote emotional balance. The limbic system keeps us in touch with the senses, the body, the emotions—through limbic activation we experience the full vitality of our life. However, when there is too much limbic input, we experience life as chaotic.[1] When the limbic system is overactive, a healthy prefrontal cortex releases the neurotransmitter GABA, which inhibits the activity of other neurotransmitters and balances certain hormonal activity so that our experience of the senses and emotions is less raw, more modulated.[2]

The prefrontal cortex's input and output fibers serve as a bridge between the cortical memory stores—which are our conscious memories—and the limbic storehouses of implicit memory and emotion. For this reason, the prefrontal cortex gives us a foundational capacity for integration, insight, and self-awareness. The information we take in through this process, consciously and unconsciously, has the opportunity to become integrated with other aspects of our life. This capacity for insight and self-awareness is a prerequisite for being able to come into healthy relationship with ourselves and others. It is the process through which knowledge becomes wisdom.

The prefrontal cortex is supported in this integrative work by a system of resonance circuitry that affects the direction of energy and information flow through the mind as it relates to our interpersonal awareness. This resonance circuitry represents the intentional states of others and provides the neural bandwidth for experiencing emotional resonance as an ongoing process within moment-to-moment life. I will describe these resonance systems more thoroughly since insight into these resonance systems lays bare one of those key tenets of Buddhism: the way to come into clear and compassionate relationship with others is through coming into good relationship with ourselves.

The *insula cortex* is positioned deep within the lateral fissure (a deep crevice near the center of the brain) where it makes connections to the regions of the brain that take in raw data from the senses, as well as to the prefrontal cortex.[3] Within this process, the insula cortex conveys information about the state of the body and gathers this information into a meaningful context. The insula cortex receives signals from mirror neurons in the parietal and frontal cortex areas (areas of the brain that process sensory experience); these mirror neurons map the "sensory implications of motor actions," based on the work of Daniel Siegel and other cutting-edge neuropsychologists. Through these mirror neurons, information from the sensory cortical areas is conveyed directly to the motor cortices to provide feedback on our immediate experience; it is also conveyed directly to the anterior insula. In other words, the mirror neurons are the feedback loop through which we know our own body and its relationship to the world.

This same sensory information simultaneously conveys an impression of the intentional states of others. It activates basic mechanisms of emotional resonance within our own felt experience as the insula cortex then sends this information down to the limbic system, the brainstem, and the body. This is experienced viscerally: muscles tighten or relax, our heart skips a beat or shifts into a calm rhythm. This sensory data then flows upward to the hypothalamus, which amplifies these sensations through hormones, endorphins, and other neurotransmitters. Through the actions of these neurotransmitters, we feel warmth in the presence of a newborn, focused and energized when meeting a new colleague. This visceral information from the body also moves back up again, through the brainstem to the insula cortex, which translates this information into a kinesthetic awareness of our body-state. We know our response to this new person through the felt sense of our own body. The sensory awareness that mirrors back our sensation of being embodied is the exact same awareness that registers awareness of another's feeling. Through the input of kinesthetic awareness to the prefrontal area through the insula, we sense another's feelings in our own body. Empathy can be said to be the full awareness of these body and limbic shifts; these bring about our capacity to perceive and respond.

It is essential that the mind develop its capacity to weave all these threads of information into a single cloth, an integrative awareness. The mind itself can be defined as "an embodied and relational process of energy and information." While we all have some level of integrative awareness, there is always more development that is possible. The capacity to stay open and connected to the limbic system's emotional and sensory awareness without being overwhelmed by instinctual responses is an art as well as a science—one which is surely needed in our rapidly changing world in which the amount of energy and information flowing towards us, through the ever-evolving frontiers of communication and social media, is unsurpassed.

Fortunately, our mind does have great capacity for growth towards higher states of integration. Daniel Siegel describes two kinds of integration: horizontal integration (right-left hemisphere integration via the corpus callosum, also known as bilateral integration) and vertical integration (body and limbic system with neocortex).[4] These communication channels between the body and mind, and between the right and left brain, help ground our lived experience. Through these, we can integrate the somato-emotional intelligence of the right hemisphere with the reasoning of the left hemisphere. These integrative processes allow us to relationally connect in an attuned, sensitive, and stable way.

Presence

This process of creating a strong relationship with others is thus strengthened by our own practice of embodied presence. As we strengthen our own vertical integration from the body to the limbic system to the neocortex, we can sense the flow of connection through our bodies; we can also feel, through the felt sense of our bodies, when disconnect happens and more easily restore our interpersonal connection.

The work begins with unconditional openness, being open to ourselves and to this very moment. Mind is innately sky-like, able to contain everything. The innate clarity of our mind is not diminished by the thoughts and emotions that come and go, any more than the sky is hindered by clouds. As the poet Rilke wrote:

> Let everything happen: beauty and terror
> just keep going. No feeling is final.[5]

Having established unconditional openness, we are able to witness the dynamic range of our own emotional experience as a natural phenomenon like the weather: earth, air, fire, and water. By bringing the power of our full presence to our own weather patterns, we are then also able to be present with, and to extend this healing presence and spacious awareness to, others and this world.

ATTUNEMENT

When presence is established, attuning with another is possible. We can describe attunement as an intentional deepening of our shared experience as received through the resonance circuitry, providing body-centered awareness of the other person as well as our own felt sense of the situation. *Resonance*, the felt sense of connection and rapport between two people, is then possible. Physically, when a therapist and client are in close rapport:

> heart rates align, breathing becomes in-sync, non-verbal signals emerge in waves that parallel each other and in some cases shifts in EEG findings and heart rate variability can occur. The functions of our autonomic nervous system . . . become aligned as we resonate with each other.[6]

Within the flow of conversation, verbal and nonverbal communication reinforces a sense of being heard and felt. That experience of resonance is experienced beneath the surface of conscious awareness first: on the subjective, physical level. This level of resonance depends on our own capacity for natural openness and whole-body connection. When our capacity to meet our own emotional weather patterns within the sky-like openness of mind is unconditional, our middle prefrontal cortex is steadfast in connecting to our limbic system. Somato-emotional information coming in can be perceived and experienced without shutting down and without reacting. This gives us the capacity to see, hear, and touch another person with the felt quality of intimacy. This sense of connection is truly needed in our world at this present time. The excesses of our time—conspicuous consumption, addiction, anomie—can be clearly seen to be rooted in two cultural imbalances. First, it is rooted in an overemphasis upon cognitive knowing, which has separated reason from felt awareness—and with this, separated the knower from the known. Second, our cultural over-emphasis upon individualism compounds the sense of isolation, so that it is experienced as a hunger for connection, which causes us to look for satisfaction in all the wrong places. What, then, will make it possible to heal this illusion of separateness and restore us to the truth of our connection?

Meditation, dance, poetry, music, and other arts can be described as therapy in the service of wholeness. These practices all bring about bilateral integration, the weaving together of right hemisphere–based sensory experience and left hemispheric–based observer consciousness. Mindfulness meditation and other body-centered work supports *vertical integration,* the flow of energy and information between the central nervous system and the middle prefrontal cortex.

The grassroots work begins with developing our own capacity to experience this natural openness of our body/mind and revitalize our felt sense of wholeness. Meditation practice supports this growth. As we practice meditation—watching our breath, our body, and mind become one—inside and outside become one. We and our life become one. This makes it possible to be one with the life force that moves through us, to trust our deepest experience and to find the courage to stay with this direct experience without adding anything and without repressing. As we come into this level of alignment, sacred space is created. Our self-empathy and inner spaciousness become the sacred circle through which we perceive and meet our world.

As this level of somato-emotional awareness cleanses our perceptions, it brings subterranean levels of knowing to the surface of consciousness. In cultivating higher awareness, the key is *awareness*: being embodied, paying attention. Coming fully to our senses through mindfulness meditation helps us develop a greater level of intimacy with our body and mind, so this is possible.

Since we know that our bodies/minds attune to other bodies/minds, the inner freedom and wholeness, which we experience through practices of mindfulness, inherently shifts the world around us—creating a greater collective capacity for compassion and insight. As Jon Kabat-Zinn has said to me, this has the potential to bring about a complete renaissance. By being the change we seek, we begin to create a mindful society. Our own moment-to-moment embodiment of compassion and insight creates new possibilities for all of us within this unbroken circle of our world.

Epilogue

ONE CONTINUOUS PRACTICE—TRY MIND

The deep curiosity regarding practices of conscious living and heightened compassion for others, which so many of us are now experiencing, are gifts that support our journeys of awakening; these are simultaneously an individuation process and our collective return to wholeness. As we reintegrate these ways of knowing, which touch the deep wholeness within us, we feel and know the truth of our connection. Out of this, compassion arises, and we engage with the unique calling and destiny that arises for each of us at this turning point of history. Our own inner work then supports the evolution of our society and healing of this earth.

This is a journey to wholeness rather than perfection. That ideal state of perfection is never achieved. Every cell in our body, every facet of our being, is always changing—just as every leaf in the forest is changing, through various hues of green. We are always in the process of becoming.

Therefore, we should be kind to ourselves and to others. And we should keep in mind that every thought, every word, every action makes a difference. By seeing the wholeness in ourselves and others, we are strengthening these luminous threads of connection. Just as a sand mandala is created grain by grain, through the moment-to-moment practice of mindful and compassionate action, we are living our way into an enlightened world. These practices of compassion are an expression of wisdom, a recognition of that original nature that we are. Sometimes we can completely do it, and sometimes we can't. That's okay. As my teacher would say, keep "try mind" and a great question—then you are on the path. It is the same as if you have already arrived. Just continue ten thousand years, nonstop. That means, give yourself completely to this moment.

On one occasion, a newspaper reporter said to my teacher Maha Ghosananda, "In your long and eventful life, you must have had many special moments."

"Yes," Maha Ghosananda replied.

"Which ones?" asked the reporter.

"Every moment," Maha Ghosananda answered.

My wish for you is that you live each moment fully, discovering within it the seeds of awakened heart. Then the joy of creation holds us in its embrace. We meet the moment as a friend. Every person we meet is our sister, our brother—the moment itself is our teacher. We rediscover that from the beginning we and the universe are never separate. This practice is simply a way of rediscovering that luminous awareness that we are—a welcoming home. *Namaste.*

—Ji Hyang Padma

Appendix
THE FIVE PRECEPTS

These five precepts offer us a way to embody the Zen path of awakening in everyday life. As we practice these precepts, it becomes easier to travel lightly, to see our interdependence, and to develop self-insight.

1. To abstain from taking life.
2. To abstain from lying.
3. To abstain from taking things not given.
4. To abstain from intoxicants, taken to the point of heedlessness.
5. To abstain from sexual misconduct.

Notes

Introduction

1. Thich Nhat Hanh, *Being Peace* (Berkeley, CA: Parallax Press, 2005), 22.
2. Zen Master Un Mun, *The Gateless Barrier*, trans. Robert Aitken (New York: Macmillan, 1991), 127.
3. Bonnie Badenoch, *Being a Brain-Wise Therapist* (New York: Norton, 2008), 52-63.
4. Cui Shaoxuan, "Black Hair and Red Cheeks: For How Long?" in *Women in Praise of the Sacred*, ed. Jane Hirshfield (New York: Harper Collins, 1995), 76.

Chapter 1. Bringing Forth That Which is Within

1. Jakusho Kwong Roshi, "Confidence in Your Original Nature," *Mountain Wind: Sonoma Mountain Zen Center Newsletter* (Summer 1995).
2. *The Gospel of Thomas*, trans. Thomas O. Lambdin (Charleston, SC: Forgotten Books, 2007).

Chapter 2. An Unbroken Circle, An Undivided Prayer

1. "Atomic Education Urged by Einstein," *New York Times*, May 25, 1946.

2. Carl Jung, *Mandala Symbolism* (Princeton, NJ: Princeton University Press, 1973), 73.

3. Khenchen Thrangu Rinpoche, *The Five Buddha Families and the Eight Consciousnesses* (Auckland, NZ: Zhyisil Chokyi Ghatsal Publications, 2001), 1.

4. Detlef Ingo Lauf, *Tibetan Sacred Art: The Heritage of Tantra* (Boston: Shambhala, 1976), 119.

5. Pabongka Rinpoche, Trijang Rinpoche, and Michael Richards, *Liberation in the Palm of Your Hand: A Concise Discourse on the Path to Enlightenment* (Somerville, MA: Wisdom Publications, 2008), 178.

Chapter 3. Hope

1. Zen Master Dae Kwang, "Thousand Year Treasure," in *Providence Zen Center Newsletter* (Cumberland, RI: Providence Zen Center, 1998), http://www.kwanumzen.org/1998/thousand-year-treasure/.

2. Coleman Barks, trans., "Childhood Friends," in *The Essential Rumi* (New York: Harper Collins, 1995), 142.

3. The author gained this understanding in conversation with His Holiness the Fourteenth Dalai Lama.

Chapter 4. The Lion's Roar

1. Chogyam Trungpa, "Mahayana: The Lion's Roar," in *The Essential Chogyam Trungpa* (Boston: Shambhala, 1999), 123–126.

2. Dainin Katagiri Roshi with Yūkō Conniff and Willa Hathaway, *Returning to Silence* (Boston: Shambhala, 1988), 72.

Chapter 5. Empathy

1. "The Metta Sutra," in *Old Pond Mind Zen Temple Sutra Book* (North Truro, MA: Pond Village Zendo, 1998), 10.

2. Adapted from Tara Brach, *Radical Acceptance: Embracing Your Life with the Heart of a Buddha* (New York: Bantam, 2004), 280.

Chapter 6. Spring Cleaning— Traveling Lightly

1. Bishop Steven Charleston, "Address" (presentation, Boston Clergy and Religious Leaders' Group for Interfaith Dialogue, Boston, May 21, 2006).

2. Nawang Khechog, "Awakening Kindness" (workshop, Wellesley College, Wellesley, MA, April 15, 2009).

Chapter 7. Indra's Net—See the Connections

1. Nawang Khechog, "Awakening Kindness" (workshop, Wellesley College, Wellesley, MA, April 15, 2009).

Chapter 8. Applied Zen—Creating the World Around Us

1. Eihei Dogen, "Mountains and Rivers Sutra," in *Moon in a Dewdrop*, trans. Tanahashi, Kazuaki (San Francisco: North Point), 102.

2. Michelle McDonald, "Emotions—Working with Anger," in *Buddhanet*, http://www.buddhanet.net/emotions.htm.

3. Rainer Maria Rilke, *Letters to a Young Poet*, trans. Stephen Mitchell (New York: Modern Library, 2001), 92.

Chapter 9. Taste and See

1. Denise Levertov, "Taste and See," in *O Taste and See* (New York: New Directions, 1964), 52.

Chapter 10. Creativity

1. Agnes De Mille, *The Life and Work of Martha Graham* (New York: Random House, 1991), 264.

2. James Hillman, *The Soul's Code* (New York: Warner, 1996), 40.

3. Daniel Siegel, "2010 Sonnabend Lecture" (presentation, Lesley University, 2010).

4. John O'Donohue, *Beauty: The Invisible Embrace* (New York: Harper Perennial, 2005), 7–8.

Chapter 11. Authenticity

1. Shunryu Suzuki, *Zen Mind, Beginner's Mind* (Boston: Shambhala, 2010), 2.

2. Zen Master Seung Sahn, *Compass of Zen* (Boston: Shambhala, 1997), 321.

3. Kobun Chino Roshi, "A Natural Action" (unpublished lecture as cited by Zenkei Blanche Hartmann, 2000, retrieved from http://www.chzc.org/hartman3.htm).

4. Bernard Glassman, "Make Me One with Everything," in *Buddhadharma*, Summer 2011, http://www.thebuddhadharma.com/web-archive/2011/5/16/make-me-one-with-everything.html.

Chapter 12. Ecology of Mind

Epigraph: Burton Watson, trans., *The Lotus Sutra* (New York: Columbia University Press, 1993), 101.

1. Eihei Dogen, "Genjo Koan," in *Pond Village Chanting Book* (North Truro, MA: Pond Village Zendo, 1998).

2. These reflections were inspired by a Dharma talk given by Seido Lee de Barros at Green Gulch Farm.

Chapter 13. Encountering the Sacred Feminine

1. Thomas Cleary, *Twilight Goddess: Spiritual Feminism and Feminist Spirituality* (Boston: Shambhala, 2002), 9.

2. Grace Schireson, Christina Feldman, Rita Gross, and Lamaa Palden Drolma, "Making Our Way—On Women and Buddhism," in *Buddhadharma*, Winter 2010, http://bdtest1.squarespace.com/web-archive/2010/11/11/forum-making-our-way-on-women-and-buddhism.html.

3. Judith Simmer-Brown, *Dakini's Warm Breath: The Feminine Principle in Tibetan Buddhism* (Boston: Shambhala, 2002), 209.

4. Red Pine, trans. *Heart Sutra* (Berkeley, CA: Counterpoint, 2005), 11.

CHAPTER 14. INYOUN—CAUSE AND EFFECT

1. Iyeoka Ivie Okoawo, "Conversation with God" (presentation, Women's Leadership Experience, Cambridge College, June 2008). This poem can also be found on Okoawo's recording, "Hum the Baseline."

CHAPTER 15. LISTEN

1. C. G. Jung, *Psychological Reflections* (Princeton, NJ: Princeton University Press, 1970), 5.

2. Hans-Georg Gadamer, as quoted in O'Donohue, *Beauty: The Invisible Embrace* (New York: Harper Perennial, 2005), 8.

3. John Tarrant, *Bring Me the Rhinoceros and Other Zen Koans That Will Save Your Life* (Boston: Shambhala, 2008), 93.

4. David Wagoner, "Lost," in *Riverbed* (Bloomington, IN: University of Indiana Press, 1972), 75.

Chapter 16. Dakini, Sky Dancer

1. Judith Simmer-Brown, *Dakini's Warm Breath: The Feminine Principle in Tibetan Buddhism* (Boston: Shambhala, 2002).

Chapter 17. Applied Zen— Compassion in Action

1. Traditional Hopi poem, as heard around a campfire by the author.
2. Sogyal Rinpoche, *The Tibetan Book of Living and Dying* (San Francisco: Harper, 1994), 358.

Chapter 18. Interpersonal Mindfulness— Zen and Relationships

1. Christine Page, "The Soul Directed Approach" (practitioner training workshop, Providence, RI: June 2001).

Chapter 19. Wholeness and the Implicate Order

1. Parker Palmer, "Keynote" (presentation, Uncovering the Heart of Higher Education Conference, San Francisco, 2007).

2. Fritjof Capra, *The Tao of Physics* (Boston: Shambhala, 2010), 311–313.

3. David Bohm, cited in Sogyal Rinpoche, *The Tibetan Book of Living and Dying* (San Francisco: Harper, 1994), 353.

4. Shi-tou Hsi-chien, "Sandokai," in *San Francisco Zen Center Chanting Book* (San Francisco: San Francisco Zen Center).

5. Palmer, *Keynote.*

CHAPTER 20. WRITING WITH WATER

1. Carlos Casteneda, *A Separate Reality* (New York: Washington Square Press, 1991), 84.

2. Jinpa Thupten, interview, *Morning Edition*, NPR, January 23, 2006.

3. Stan Lombard, "Respecting Our Ancestral Practice: The Morning Bell Chant, Part I," in *Primary Point* 19, no. 2 (Summer 2001): 10–14.

4. Madeleine Ko-In Bastis, *Peaceful Dwelling* (Boston: Tuttle, 2000).

CHAPTER 21. PRACTICES OF RECIPROCITY AND GRATITUDE

Epigraph: Stephanie Flanders, as spoken at a ceremony attended by the author.

1. Zen Master Seung Sahn, "Earth, Air, Fire, Water: Repaying the Universe," in *Primary Point*, Winter 1990.

2. Evelyn Rysdyk, "Creating Conscious Crossroads," in *Sacred Hoop* (Autumn 2004): 22–25.

3. His Holiness the Fourteenth Dalai Lama, in conversation with the author.

CHAPTER 22. MAKING THE CONNECTIONS: ZEN AND THE MIND

1. Daniel Siegel, *Mindsight* (New York: Bantam, 2010).

2. John E. Mendoza and Anne L. Foundas, *Clinical Neuroanatomy: A Neurobehavioral Approach* (New York: Springer, 2008).

3. Ibid., 306–7.

4. Daniel Siegel, *The Mindful Brain* (New York: Norton, 2007).

5. Joanna Macy and Anita Barrows, trans., *Rilke's Book of Hours: Love Poems to God* (New York: Riverhead Trade, 2005), 88.

6. Daniel Siegel, *The Mindful Therapist* (New York: Norton, 2010), 57.

GLOSSARY

For the reader's convenience, the glossary is divided into two parts: one for Buddhist terms and one for neuropsychological terms.

BUDDHIST TERMS

Avalokitesvara: Sanskrit name for the Bodhisattva of compassion. See Kwan Seum Bosal.

Bardo: Intermediate space between this life and the next.

Bodhicitta: Awakened heart/mind.

Bodhissatva: An archetype of compassion. Traditionally described as an awakened being who stays in the world, rather than transcending it, in order to relieve suffering and benefit all beings. Alt: Someone who has the compassionate direction to be of service.

Bodhissatva Vow: The commitment of a Bodhisattva to fully realize compassion, life after life, until all beings are saved from suffering.

Buddha: Awakened one. Refers to the historical Shakyamuni Buddha, Siddharta Gutama; to the awakened beings who have come before and after; and to the original nature we all possess, which is clear, compassionate, and wise.

Chitta: Unconscious memory.

Dakini: In Buddhism, a feminine principle that serves as a protector of the teachings; may also be an enlightened female being who transmits the teaching. Associated with the element of space, the quality of emptiness, primordial energy, and sky-like mind.

Dharma: Truth, the nature of things, phenomena. Refers to the teaching of the Buddha, as this reflects natural law.

Dharma Talk: A traditional Zen teaching shared within the context of a formal talk.

Dōgen: Founder of the Soto school within Japanese Zen; wrote many texts that are recognized as seminal.

Don't-know mind: In Korean Zen, used to refer to the mind before thinking, before concepts and attachments, which is as open and spacious as the sky.

Dzogchen: A body of teachings within Tibetan Buddhism that aims at actualizing the natural state of wisdom and clear compassion.

Form and emptiness: In Buddhism, *form* refers to the tangible shapes energy takes in the world to bring about all phenomena: the physical world and explicit ways of knowing. *Emptiness* refers to that energy that underlies all things, out of which everything arises and to which everything returns; it is connected with tacit ways of knowing. The interplay of form and emptiness is witnessed through the ephemeral nature of all phenomena, which come and go like waves upon the ocean.

Forty-nine day ceremony: Ceremony performed forty-nine days after death, which is considered more significant than the immediate memorial service, as it is believed that a person completes the intermediate state of the bardo at forty-nine days, and enters a new life.

Hopchang: An expression of respect, hands palm-to-palm.

Immeasurables: Four positive qualities: loving-kindness, sympathetic joy, compassion, and equanimity, which are considered limitless.

Indra: In Hinduism, king of the gods.

Inyoun: The cause-and-effect that takes place over lifetimes, and can produce close connections when two people have just met.

Ji Jang Bosal/Jizo: The Bodhissatva of compassion who guides the deceased and illuminates their journey through the intermediate state of the bardo into new life. Known as Ksitigarbha in Sanskrit.

Kali Yuga: The fourth age of the world according to Hindu cosmology. It is associated with discord, an age in which it will be challenging to stay true to one's principles.

Kido: A chanting meditation practice undertaken for a certain period of time, or a chanting retreat.

Koan: A teaching tool used within Zen practice to test and clarify a student's understanding. These pose a dilemma that cannot be solved by the rational, analytical mind:

an answer must be sourced from the before-thinking, nondual mind. Known as *kung-an* within Korean Zen.

Kshanti: Sanskrit for patience; implies an active quality of forbearance.

Kwan Seum Bosal: The Korean name for the Bodhissatva Avalokitesvara, also known as Kuan *Yin (Chinese)* and *Kanzeon (Japanese):* A literal translation of the Bodhissatva's name is "the one who perceives the sound of the world" (and, implicitly, its suffering) and responds spontaneously. The central archetype of the Bodhissatva, representing limitless compassion.

Lineage holder: In Buddhism, a person who has been given transmission; that is, formally recognized as a teacher in the line of transmission, which traces back to Shakyamuni Buddha.

Mandala: Within Tibetan Buddhism, a point surrounded by a traditional geometrical design that symbolizes the inner world and the macrocosm. A sacred circle that represents, simultaneously, an inner landscape and physical realm within which every element of experience is unified, balanced and complete.

Maya: (Sanskrit) The play of phenomena within constant change, upon the pure energy of nonduality, which can be envisioned as waves upon an infinite ocean.

Mudra: A traditional posture of the hands and body associated with meditation.

Namaste: "The spirit in me greets and honors the spirit in you," a common greeting and salutation upon parting in

South Asia, accompanied usually by hands palm-to-palm in respect.

Pai Chang: A great Chinese Zen Master, who lived in the eighth and ninth centuries and organized the Zen monastic rule.

Phowa practice: The Tibetan practice of preparing to attain the highest level of awareness while transitioning through death

Prajna: Nondual wisdom; wisdom that sees beyond appearance to the essence of things.

Prajna Paramita: Perfection of wisdom; one of the six *paramitas* (perfections) that are considered positive states which one should cultivate in order to awaken. Also commonly refers to the Prajna Paramita Sutra, which describes the Buddhist teaching of nonduality.

Prostration: A meditation practice of bowing with one's whole body, so that the entire body is brought to the ground in a gesture of respect.

Roshi: An honorific used in Japanese Zen to denote a teacher who provides spiritual guidance to a community, usually implies formal certification as a lineage holder.

Samskara: (Sanskrit) Memory trace that surfaces in conscious awareness.

Sangha: Community. Refers to the original assembly of monks and nuns, to Buddhist temple and meditation center communities, and to all beings since all beings are ultimately part of our family.

Sunim: Honorific used in Korean Buddhism to refer to a monk or nun.

Sutra: Traditionally refers to a record of the teaching of the historical Buddha, or another highly revered ancestral Buddhist teacher.

Tandien: A point three fingers below the navel, which is considered the center of one's physical and spiritual energy. The place where the full energy within the breath is received, a source of strength and will. Literally translated from Korean as "energy garden."

Tashi tendrel: Auspicious connections; auspicious coincidence based on the interplay of cause-and-effect, whether visible or unseen. Comes from the teaching on pratitya-samutpada, the law of cause and effect.

Vesica piscis: A shape within sacred geometry defined as the ground where, with two equal circles, the circumference of one circle meets the center of the other. This creates a shape that resembles the shape of a fish.

Yogi: A dedicated meditation practitioner within certain Vipassana and Tibetan schools of Buddhism.

Neuropsychological Terms

Amygdala: A small, almond-shaped region of the brain that is part of the limbic system and affects fear responses, memory, and emotional learning.

Brainstem: The lower region of the brain, which links with the spinal cord, conducting energy and information between the brain and the body. It integrates body-brain functions, and thus regulates the cardiovascular system, the respiratory system, sensitivity, awareness, and consciousness.

Hippocampus: A region of the brain that is part of the limbic system. Its functions include memory and spatial awareness.

Hypothalamus: A part of the brain that connects the nervous system to the endocrine system. The hypothalamus affects body temperature, hunger, thirst, fatigue, sleep, and circadian rhythms.

Insula cortex: A part of the brain situated deep in the sulcus between the temporal lobe and the frontal lobe that affects emotion. Its functions include perception motor control, self-awareness, cognitive function, and interpersonal experience.

Interoception: Our felt awareness of our viscera, muscles, ventral nerve, and other inner sensations.

Limbic system: The interconnected structures in the brain that support emotion, behavior, and memory functions; a significant part of the body/mind feedback loop.

Neocortex: The newest part of the brain to evolve; functions include thought and language, spatial reasoning, sensory perception, and motor commands. Includes the prefrontal cortex.

Neurotransmitter: A chemical that transmits signals from a neuron to a target cell across a synapse (gap). Many of these affect our arousal level and emotions.

Prefrontal cortex: An area in the front of the brain that is associated with higher functions, such as insight, attunement, emotional effective balance, fear modulation, empathy, ethics, and intuition.

INDEX

Index

Index

Index

Index

CREDITS

Grateful acknowledgment is made for permission
to reproduce the following material:

Page 3   "In Vietnam" reprinted from *Being Peace* (2005) by Thich Nhat Hanh with permission of Parallax Press, Berkeley, California. www.parallax.org

Page 5   "Spring comes with Flowers" by Zen Master Wu-Men, translated by Robert Aitken, appears by permission of Honolulu Diamond Sangha.

Page 17   Two lines of Cui Shaoxuan's [p.76] from *Women in Praise of the Sacred*, edited by Jane Hirshfield. Copyright © 1994 by Jane Hirshfield. Reprinted by permission of HarperCollins Publishers.

Page 41   "Don't turn your head. Keep looking at the bandaged place" from *The Essential Rumi*, trans. Coleman Barks, copyright 1995 appears by permission of Coleman Barks.

Pages 56–57   Metta meditation appears by permission of Tara Brach.

Page 61   Bishop Steven Charleston's address to the Boston Clergy and Religious Leaders' Group appears by permission of Bishop Steven Charleston.

Page 84   "How could we forget those ancient myths" by Rainer Maria Rilke, trans. Stephen Mitchell, © 1993. Reprinted by arrangement with Shambhala Publications, Inc., Boston MA. www.shambhala.com.

Page 87   "Taste and See" by Denise Levertov, *O Taste and See*, copyright 1964 by New Directions.

Page 105   "The rain falls everywhere," from *Lotus Sutra*, trans. Burton Watson, copyright 1993 by Columbia University Press. Reprinted by permission of the publisher.

Page 123   "Blink of an Eye" by Iyeoka Ivie Okoawo, copyright 2007 by Iyeoka Ivie Okoawo. Reprinted by permission of Iyeoka Ivie Okoawo.

Page 132   "Lost" by David Wagoner, *Riverbed*, copyright 1972 by University of Illinois Press.

Page 165   Meditation, *Peaceful Dwelling*, Madeline Ko-i Bastis, Copyright ©2000, Madeline Ko-i Bastis. Reproduced by permission of Tuttle Publishing.

Page 181   "Let everything happen," by Rainer Maria Rilke copyright 1996 by Joanna Macy. Reprinted by permission of Joanna Macy.

Quest Books

encourages open-minded inquiry into
world religions, philosophy, science, and the arts
in order to understand the wisdom of the ages,
respect the unity of all life, and help people explore
individual spiritual self-transformation.

Its publications are generously supported by
The Kern Foundation,
a trust committed to Theosophical education.

Quest Books is the imprint of
the Theosophical Publishing House,
a division of the Theosophical Society in America.
For information about programs, literature,
on-line study, membership benefits, and international centers,
see www.theosophical.org
or call 800-669-1571 or (outside the U.S.) 630-668-1571.

Related Quest Titles

The Boundless Circle: Caring for Creatures and Creation,
by Michael W. Fox

Breathe into Being: Awakening to Who You Really Are,
by Dennis Lewis

Everyday Dharma: Seven Weeks to Finding the Buddha in You,
by Lama Willa Miller

The Meditative Path, by John Cianciosi

*Questions from the City, Answers from the Forest:
Simple Lessons You Can Use from a Western Buddhist Monk,*
by Ajahn Sumano Bhikkhu

A Still Forest Pool: The Insight Meditation of Achaan Chah,
by Jack Kornfield, with Paul Breiter

To order books or a complete Quest catalog,
call 800-669-9425 or (outside the U.S.) 630-665-0130.

ABOUT THE AUTHOR

Ji Hyang Padma serves as Director of Spirituality and Education Programs and Buddhist chaplain at Wellesley College. She also teaches at Babson College, Omega Institute, and Esalen Institute. Ji Hyang Padma has done intensive Zen training and teaching in Asia and North America for twenty years, fifteen of these as a nun in the Chogye Zen tradition.

Ji Hyang has also served as Abbot of Cambridge Zen Center, as well as a meditation teacher at Harvard University and Boston University. She is currently completing a PhD in psychology with a specialization in transpersonal psychology. Her research focuses on ancient and contemporary Buddhist healing practices. Her writing has appeared recently in *My Neighbor's Faith: Stories of Interreligious Encounter, Growth, and Transformation* and *Arts of Contemplative Care: Pioneering Voices in Buddhist Chaplaincy and Pastoral Work*. Her work can be accessed through these websites:

Natural Wisdom: *http://www.natural-wisdom.org*
Natural Wisdom blog: *http://naturalwisdom.blogspot.com*

More Praise for Ji Hyang Padma's
Living the Season

"In practicing Zen, nothing beats the practice. Ji Hyang's new book, *Living the Season*, is exceptional in focusing on just that and not in indulging in conceptual fantasies about Zen—she gives us a cup of tea instead of just talk about tea, a cup of tea she hands us to taste for ourselves."

—Red Pine, celebrated author and translator

"Ji Hyang's words are a flowing meditation in mindfulness. Her writing is poetic and magnetic, each page being wrapped in wisdom and practical teachings for change and transformation at a soul and spirit level. Refreshing, enlightening, and deeply restorative."

—Jackee Holder, author of *Soul Purpose* and *49 Ways to Write Yourself Well*

"*Living the Season* is like a flower that opens in your hands, reminding you to dissolve into the grace of each moment. Ji Hyang offers a lucid picture of Zen and of how it applies to us, today, now, with simple techniques that are each like a haiku of wisdom."

—Brett Bevell, author of *America Needs a Buddhist President*, *Reiki for Spiritual Healing*, and *New Reiki Software for Divine Living*

"*Living the Season* is a wise and lyrical introduction to meditation practice and mindful living. We as individuals, as a nation, and as inhabitants of Planet Earth are all transforming—whether we find it comfortable or not. A former Buddhist nun and current Interfaith Advisor at Wellesley College, Padma offers both historical perspective and practical guidance for living a more present life in the midst of change and challenge. What Martin Luther King, Jr., said about Thich Nhat Hanh's writings also holds true for Padma's: her 'ideas for peace, if applied, would build a monument to ecumenism, to world [brother and sisterhood], to humanity.'"

—Susan Elia MacNeal,
author of *Wedding Zen*

"A smart and practical guide for making Zen a part of your everyday life. Read it and be transformed!"
—Lama Willa Miller, teacher at the National Dharma
Fellowship and author of *Everyday Dharma:
Seven Weeks to Finding the Buddha in You*

"Ji Hyang Padma has superbly brought an ancient living wisdom into our modern world in the writing of this book. Her accessible and practical strategies are guaranteed to awaken your soul, connect you to yourself, and transform your life. This book is a must-read for our busy and troubled times."

—Robert Ohotto, author of
Transforming Fate into Destiny